Challenges of the Heart

Challenges of the Heart

by Cynthia Powers Miller

Challenges of the Heart

by Cynthia Powers Miller

©1991 Word Aflame Press
Hazelwood, MO 63042

Cover Design by Tim Agnew

All Scripture quotations in this book are from the King James Version of the Bible unless otherwise identified.

Printed in United States of America.

Printed by

Library of Congress Cataloging-in-Publication Data

Miller, Cynthia Powers.
    Challenges of the heart / Cynthia Powers Miller.
        p.   cm.
    ISBN 0-932581-79-X
    1. Marriage—Religious aspects—Christianity. 2. Family
3. Miller, Cynthia Powers.   I. Title.
BV835.M56 1991
248.8'44—dc20   90-21432
                                         CIP

Because you have loved me with a committed love, believed in me even when you didn't understand me, and counseled and consoled me with godly wisdom and insight . . . I dedicate this book to you, my beloved husband and best friend, Stanton E. Miller.

Contents

Foreword

The glamorous myth of a perfect spouse can blind men and women to the realities of coping with the everyday stress of married life. Though undertaken with all sincerity and high hopes, an attempt to rebuild lives in a second marriage often ends in tragedy. The agonies of single parenthood prompt many remarriages, but then the multiple problems of hurting, emotionally scarred children sometimes help to sink the frail boat of hoped-for marital happiness.

Against the somber reality of failed marriages that has touched many families, how satisfying to see a couple who has made marriage work! My visit in Cindy's home provided insight into how sweetly King Jesus can build a Christian home on a foundation of love and respect.

Cindy has written with candor, complete honesty, and competent spiritual understanding on a delicate subject that urgently needs airing. She offers hope and practical guidelines for voyagers on the sea of matrimony—especially when it is the second time around for one of the partners.

I highly recommend this book written out of a valiant heart. It is based on the eternal Word of God that is forever settled in heaven and that is guaranteed to change lives on earth.

Nona Freeman

Preface

Because of sin, we live in a world where death and divorce step into hearts and homes, tearing families apart. Although such tragedies were not part of God's original plan for the human race, He has made provisions for healing and comforting broken families. According to Psalm 68:6, "God setteth the solitary in families."

Some situations result from sin or wrong choices before a person was saved, some result from sin or wrong choices after a person was saved, and some result from tragedies beyond a person's control. Regardless of the reasons or of past rights and wrongs, these marriages and families need help, and it is God's will for them to function properly and be successful. This book is written to help address this need, which is very real in our world today.

In broken families, gaps are left where a parent or spouse used to be. There is a need—a void to be filled. That filled void is known to the world as "Bill's second wife" or "Jenny's stepmom." For a first-time bride these designations seem very negative. She is always second! She must come to realize that being second does not mean being second best.

Before I married, a minister's wife told me that she was concerned for me and to expect adjustments and difficulties. This wise woman was trying to help me, but I, in my love-filled bliss, sailed past her warnings.

Nine or ten months later I called her back. This time it was different. I needed her wisdom and sought her advice.

"Why didn't you tell me what it would be like?" I asked her. After all, she had been in a similar situation as a new bride.

"Cindy, I told you it would be difficult," her gentle voice reminded me.

"You said difficult—not heartbreaking!" I replied, half joking and half serious. We talked for over an hour, and this time I really listened.

I do not have all the answers, but experience is a great teacher.

"For as he thinketh in his heart, so is he" (Proverbs 23:7). The heart—the center of our emotions—is our mind. A bride whose husband married previously faces challenges every day. Her emotions are challenged to accept her spouse's previous love with understanding and without jealousy, to love another's child as her own, to blend and bond with an established family and not feel like an outsider or visitor, to accept as her friends and family people who were part of her husband's previous marriage. Not only is all of this required of her, but she is expected to carry it out graciously.

The following pages are a collection of lessons that God has taught me and experiences that other women in a first-time marriage with a second-time partner have willingly shared. Many have asked that their names be kept confidential.

Out of respect for the privacy of the women who participated, their names and the names of their family members have been changed. The situations, their stories, and their advice remain the same.

I challenge you to read with an open heart!

Acknowledgements

Without the very special people who cooperated with me in every way this book would not be a reality. I would like to express my love and appreciation to them all.

Thank you, April, Jonathan, and Nathan, for allowing me to spend time alone in writing and for looking after each other while I did so. You are my precious gifts from God.

Mother and Dad, your consistent example of Christian living, faith in a great God, and prayer has been my stronghold. Mere words could not express my love for you.

Donna, being your sister is a honor. I treasure you and all that you have taught me through the years. Your contributions to this book are too numerous to mention, but God knows and will reward you in His generous way. Bless you!

"A friend loveth at all times" (Proverbs 17:17). I'm thankful for the love encouragement, and support of my friends . . . Glenda Andrus, Jelaine Lumpkin, and Dayle Shockley.

Annette Schweiger, everyone needs an "Ethel" in her life. You are more than my friend; you are my armor-bearer.

And a very special thank you to Billie Marie Johnson, my friend, teacher, and traveling companion. I know you introduced me to Stan so you could stay home for a while! Because you listened to that "still small voice," God's perfect will was accomplished.

1 ♥♥♥♥♥♥♥♥♥♥

Falling in Love

Someone told me that a relief pitcher is allowed eight warm-up pitches when he comes into a baseball game. In life, when we enter a marriage we are not allowed tryouts or warm-ups to prepare us for the "game." When we marry we are put directly into the game, and that game is the most important one we will ever play.

To avoid the obvious is easy. It is the hidden obstacles that are dangerous. It is the unexpected curve in the road that causes accidents. We can compare marriage to a highway that is always under construction—always being improved—for it takes work to make it a success.

A marriage does not come heaven made. It takes two people striving and willing to give one hundred percent of themselves to better each other. Some people say that marriage is fifty-fifty, but I disagree. I say that for a marriage to be successful, both partners must be willing to give one hundred percent. Some days you may be giving eighty percent and your husband twenty percent or vice versa, but those days balance out. It is your willingness to give that is so important.

In this chapter we will investigate the hidden obstacles that two people will almost certainly encounter in a marriage when one of them has been married previously. These are the areas that you may think will take care of themselves, but before the honeymoon is over you may be forced to deal with these issues. Wouldn't it be better to deal with them now and be free to enjoy the honeymoon?

Building upon Broken Dreams

The first thing to realize is that your marriage is very special. Perhaps you have watched your friends marry and start new lives and you think you have it all figured out. But unless your friends married into ready-made families also, then you cannot base your plans on their experiences. It is not an accurate guideline for you to follow.

If you have fallen in love and pledged your life to a man who has been through a heartbreak, you must realize that he has faced the ultimate hurt in life—the loss of a much-loved wife. If he lost his wife because death snatched her away from him then you will be building your life upon the broken dreams of his past. If your husband lost his first wife because sin wreaked havoc in the family, then you will be building your life upon the shattered vows of his previous marriage.

What are the results of broken dreams and shattered vows? Anger. Hurt. Rejection. Fear. Walls built around the heart to protect it from future pain. One or all of these emotions must be dealt with at some point after a death or divorce.

How the Past Affects the Present

As we drove from the Sydney, Australia, airport to Canberra, where we would be staying for a few days, a discussion of marriage, the pros and cons, was well under way. This seems to be a common debate between the happily married and the happily single. A hundred miles and several kangaroos later, the debate changed to a more sensitive topic. The new subject matter could have been titled "Which Hurts Worse—Death or Divorce?" My husband was positive that death was the most painful way to lose a spouse, while Ellen was convinced that divorce was more painful. Both were defending their views because of what they had suffered.

Stan: In death your love is snatched from you.

Ellen: In divorce you must deal with rejection. Death is a natural process of nature, but divorce is unnatural and harder to accept.

Since that time I have watched this same debate between others, and I have concluded that whichever one— death or divorce—caused your spouse to hurt, whichever one caused his heart to be broken and brought grief to the one you love, then that is the worst.

Both leave scars. Both create fear to love again, fears that most newlywed couples do not have to deal with. They may be unspoken but they are there. If you have never been where your spouse has been, you cannot fully understand why he feels the way he does. Why does he still hurt over her memory if he loves you? How can he still feel sad after all these years and all your love? Why can't he fall in love and forget?

The past cannot be completely forgotten. The past has created the man you love today. If you are going to be married to a man with a past love, then you must be willing to bring the results and memories of that past love into your life. Can you forget your childhood? Can you forget your first date or first boyfriend? Can you forget a best friend who brought you years of happiness? How much of your life are you willing to pretend never existed? Several women in this situation have told me that their biggest disappointment was realizing that even though this man and marriage was their first and greatest love and commitment their spouse could not say the same. They were the only newlywed in their marriage.

The Importance of Time

The best advice for anyone who is considering a marriage relationship with a person who has just lost his spouse is . . . WAIT! There is a natural period of grief, in death or divorce, a time of sorrow over the loss. There is sorrow over the death of a spouse, or in the case of a divorce, sorrow over the death of what was once a love-filled relationship.

While in grief people take steps that they might otherwise would have never considered. Time is vital in order to make a balanced decision regarding the future. There needs to be

- time to grieve
- time to heal
- time to readjust attitudes and lifestyles without the former spouse
- time to focus on the future
- time for decisions to be made based on healthy mental attitudes
- time for the bereaved to see the potential partner as the person he or she is, not as a replacement for the spouse who was lost.

A pastor's wife shared with me a moving story that illustrates the need for this time. As a teenager she lost her mother. Her father quickly remarried. Karlyn had a difficult time understanding this apparent disloyalty to her mother. Years later her father confided to her that in his grief and sorrow he could not manage life alone. He had married his present wife thinking she would be able to fill the void created by the death of Karlyn's mother. He told Karlyn that he never took the time to know this woman because he was looking for a replacement of what he had lost. He had not considered that his new wife was an individual with a personality all her own. The result of this hasty marriage was years spent in a loveless marriage. She was the exact opposite of Karlyn's mother, yet she tried to take her place. Many tears and hurts later, there is merely acceptance where love could have been.

As much as one person may want to help another, no one can do what time can. The Bible clearly states, "To every thing there is a season, and a time to every purpose under the heaven" (Ecclesiastes 3:1). The seven verses following further define the seasons and times of life. There are definite times for rejoicing, but there must also be a time of mourning. There are negative times in life, but time will produce something positive if it is allowed to work.

Hidden Obstacles: Negative Emotions

Let us discuss some of the negative emotions that are a part of a death or divorce and that can become hidden obstacles to a new relationship.

Bitterness. The seed of bitterness can be produced by a tragedy. This little seed is hardy, and it does not take much nurturing to cause growth. It is planted in the soil of disappointment and hurt. It is watered with the tears of self-pity. The seed prospers and grows with plant food called "I Didn't Deserve This!" When a plant is produced it quickly takes over the garden of the heart, killing off the fragile little seedlings of joy, happiness, and acceptance that are struggling to grow again.

The only way to kill off this destroyer is with prayer. We must realize that God is almighty, and when our life is in His hands He will protect us and cause us to prosper. We must be willing to allow happiness and peace to take root in our heart.

Fear. This emotion can dwell in the heart of someone who is newly engaged or married. If someone has suffered a loss before, his first thought upon falling in love again is often, What if I lose this one too? The reasoning is that if it happened once it could happen again. There is a fear of loving again because of a fear of losing again.

The antidote to this fear is to do everything possible

to show your loyalty to your spouse. If you have married a man who lost his first wife, give him absolutely no reason to doubt that you love him and him only. In the event of a divorce in your husband's first marriage you must realize that his biggest hurt was rejection. Every man I talked with who had been through a divorce said that he felt the rejection of his love and as a husband was worse than if his wife had died.

This rejection can cause your husband to be jealous or to build a wall of protection around his heart. Let him know how important he is in your life. Shower him with praise. Do not compare him to other men. Give your husband every reason to trust you and no reason to mistrust you.

Anger is present in both death and divorce. In a divorce there is a specific target for this anger. If the marriage was dissolved because of a death there is no real target for that anger. Who can the surviving spouse be angry with? God? No, He is the only source of strength and hope. The spouse who died? How unreasonable; he or she did not want to die. The disease that took the life? Yes, but a person cannot plead with a disease to be merciful. No one can argue with and accuse a disease of destroying a home, a marriage, and a life. Perhaps if life ended in a car accident, the spouse could feel anger toward the driver of the other vehicle. But ultimately the survivor needs to surrender that anger to God. The time to heal is now. He should allow God to take his anger and replace it with peace and acceptance. Anger will keep a person from God. It will become a wall that blocks the healing gifts and prevents the rebuilding of a beautiful, profitable existence.

Guilt is present mostly when a widow or widower begins to think of remarrying. In my marriage my husband and I had to face the feelings of guilt that Stan felt for remarrying. He had to come to terms with his feeling of betrayal to his first marriage and his first wife.

Stan had a very happy, love-filled, seven and one-half years with his first wife. The loyalty to Cyndy and their marriage did not vanish because she died. Even though Stan knew that he had every right to marry again, that upon Cyndy's death the relationship had ended, still emotionally it was hard to put in perspective.

It takes time to feel comfortable in a new relationship, time to lose the awkwardness of loving someone new. This time frame varies. For some it may take a few weeks, while for others it may be months or years. It depends on the individual involved, the amount of time that has elapsed since the end of the marriage, and how the marriage ended.

It is difficult to feel anything but rejection when your husband feels guilty for marrying you, but please be patient with him. Once again, time will destroy emotion and replace it with confidence in a new relationship of love and marriage.

"If We Only Knew Then What We Know Now"

In an interview Dale shared some thoughts and advice for the woman marrying to a man who had been through a divorce. "If a woman is considering marriage to a man who has been married before, it is vital for her to ask lots of questions about his former relationship. This may sound strange, but by forcing him to talk about his previous wife, you may stumble onto some things about him you did not know, and may not believe. For example, a man who is divorced must share some of the responsibility for having forsaken his own vow, 'Till death do us part.' Remember, there are two sides to every story, and this is especially true in broken homes. You may feel uncomfortable asking these kinds of questions, and I certainly don't suggest asking them unless you are engaged to be married. But if you are pledged to this man, you have a right to know what went wrong. While you'll only hear his side of the story—more than likely—you'll still gain some insights as to what he expected in a wife, what he felt caused the breakup, and you'll also be able to see what made him so unhappy that he would agree to a divorce. Be prepared: this can be a very enlightening conversation. If it leads to your calling off your engagement, you are probably much better off. You should never enter into a marriage with any unanswered questions, and certainly not about his last relationship."

In either situation, death or divorce, some basic rules apply. First, love alone is not a good enough reason for marrying into a ready-made family. You should build your friendship, keep an open communication and a deep respect for each other, work out a plan for the happiness of the family, and pray about your decision until you know God has said, "Yes, this has My stamp of approval."

Get to know your future spouse. What happened in his previous marriage? Are there any deep wounds that have not healed? Is there a broken heart that has not fully mended?

Time is a healer. For the person who is suffering, that statement is hard to believe. If the one you are considering as a marriage partner has not allowed the process of healing to take place in his heart, then it is much better for you as an individual and for both of you as a couple to postpone any marriage plans. He may need your friendship now but be unable to handle the deeper commitment that is vital to a lasting and beautiful relationship. Don't push for more than he can handle. It is in your best interest to see the healing of your loved one take place. You want to be loved and needed as a partner. Do not allow yourself to be used. Unintentionally, if healing has not taken place, your future spouse could be using you to hide from the pain of his hurts.

Let him talk about his loss. Allow him to share his hurt, anger, or disappointments. Give space and time for the healing process to take place. Above all else first be a friend, a listening ear. Show that you care. True love cannot be selfish. You are in love and you want a cloud-nine experience day and night, but your partner may need to grieve. He may need time to adjust to the fact that it is acceptable to love again. It may even be difficult for him to realize that he is capable of loving again.

Do not be too quick to push a marriage relationship with someone who has just lost his spouse and has not allowed time and the Lord to produce a healing of emotions.

If you are already married to someone who is struggling with guilt, anger, bitterness, or sorrow, be patient and prayerful. Your spouse must work through these emotions before he can be free to love you fully as you desire to be loved. Again, be a friend to your spouse. Help him through his difficult adjustment. Do not become angry at him for having these feelings. You probably were aware of them before you married him. Ask God for wisdom and understanding.

Remember, this too shall pass, for time is a healer!

♥ 2 ♥♥♥♥♥♥♥♥♥♥

Making Decisions

*H*idden obstacles also can arise in a marriage as the result of lack of planning. The importance of thorough planning and discussion before marriage cannot be stressed too much.

The only way to make decisions is by discussing and planning. Stable decisions that are good for husband, wife, and children don't just happen.

Decisions regarding your future must be carefully prayed over and thought through. It is important to think about questions such as the following.

- Are you compatible?
- Are you good friends?
- Do you share the same interests?
- Do you have the same goals?
- Do you share the same love for the Lord?
- Do you have to compromise your Christian standards or beliefs in order to accommodate this relationship?

- Do you love his children or do you merely tolerate them?

The Importance of Early Discussions

Here are some very good reasons for premarital discussions about your upcoming life together.

- To avoid hurt feeling, resentment, anger, feelings of betrayal, and feelings of being deceived.
- To make sure that your marriage will be peaceful and not full of arguments over things you had assumed.
- "Can two walk together, except they be agreed?" (Amos 3:3). Discussions bring about the changes, compromises, and understanding needed to ensure togetherness in the marriage and harmony in the home.
- To eliminate frustration over things that cannot be changed. You will not be able to say, "If I had only known, I would have . . ." Once you know what to expect, by marrying this person you are saying, "I agree to accept the situation as it is." After marriage, you are at peace because you knew what to expect in advance.

Be mature enough to discuss openly and honestly every aspect of your relationship and every area of your intended life together. If you love each other enough to marry, then you should be able to be totally honest.

Do not hope for undiscussed changes, things that you plan to wait until after the marriage ceremony to bring up. If there is an area of incompatibility, lack of honest communication, or unconcern for the feelings of your future mate, then the marriage will begin poorly on a note of deception. It is deceptive not to verbalize fears, desires, or complaints. Your silence about certain matters says, "I accept you and your situation as it is. I feel no need of change."

The Danger of Assuming

Don't assume anything! If you do, you may set yourself up for major disappointments, and these disappointments could put a big strain on your new marriage.

Your new spouse is not a mind reader. He will not automatically know that you want or need certain things in your marriage.

Don't set yourself up to be hurt! If you see an area that is potentially harmful, point it out to your spouse. Don't allow him to walk into a trap.

Don't assume your husband is doing something because he loved his first wife more than he loves you. If you are concerned about an action of his, ask him, "Why are you doing this? What are the reasons for your decision?" It may surprise you how much he cares for you and is trying to do his very best for you.

Don't assume your husband knows when people say things that hurt you. If someone negatively compares you to his first wife or criticizes you as a mother, it is O.K. to say "I hurt because . . ." Don't make him guess.

Don't assume your spouse will never love you like he loved before. There is a very real need in all of us to be loved and needed. Love him and allow him to love you in a special "yours and mine," "not to be compared" way.

This is a one-of-a-kind relationship. Each relationship is unique. Like snowflakes, no two are the same.

To assume something is unfair to your spouse. In doing so you act as judge and juror, passing sentence before the accused has had a chance to defend himself.

The Importance of Communication

Here are a few examples of problems that can arise from lack of discussion and planning.

An important question to consider is Where will you live? His house, furniture, and decor all reflect the woman who used to live in his home. How do you feel about using her things? Will you feel like a guest in your own home? Is it financially feasible for you to replace the furnishings or buy a new home? If finances are a deterrent to plans of moving or refurnishing, what will you do to make this place a home for you? If children are involved, you can't wipe out their identity in trying to establish your own. Do you have a plan for gradual change or is your idea that of "She came, she saw, she conquered"?

My husband and I thought we had communicated in this area, but how wrong we were. My husband said, "The house is yours. You can do with it whatever you want, but the garage is mine." Visions of shopping and decorating filled my head. My dream home began to materialize in my brain. I was ready to begin. I had first-time marriage thinking! I was a new bride. New brides get to go shopping and pick out furniture and carpet and drapes and . . .

When reality dawned on me I was shocked. He didn't mean redecorate the house. He meant rearrange the existing furniture. Put a picture up. Paint a wall. Simple things like that. The result of our miscommunication was hurt. He felt hurt that I would expect so much by wanting to put a financial burden on him. On my part I felt cheated. I had planned on getting to do all the things my sister and friends had done. I assumed I was in agreement with him. When my little world was shattered I was left trying to deal with my resentment.

When you are disappointed you feel resentful. Resentment can turn to anger and anger to bitterness. Logic can understand finances, but at a time of hurt and disappointment who wants to be logical? This misunderstanding could have been easily avoided if we had not assumed so much.

Janet: It is important to discuss in detail the subject of adding children to the existing family. I was worried about Ron's children accepting me. The unknown is frightening, and I didn't want to deal with it. Ron took me at my word. After my expression of doubt over the wisdom or even the necessity of our adding to the family the subject was closed. In Ron's mind we would not be having any children. Later in our marriage, when I finally convinced him that I wanted a baby, he had a closed mind about it. Ron eventually agreed to our having a baby, but only on the condition that we would only have one child. I resented that. Why did I have to be the wife to be told one and no more?

Regina: Here is an unusual problem. My husband plans to be buried by his first wife when he dies. That hurts my feelings. I know when I die it won't matter, but as long as I'm alive it hurts my feelings. It seems, though my husband tells me it is not, that he is saying she is and will always be first to him.

I feel possessive and rejected at the same time. I want to be by him even in death, and he doesn't want me. This is another example of feeling that I am his second choice. He is only with me because he can't be with his real love.

If we had thought to discuss this before marriage and he had made his intentions known, then I could have chosen to accept the situation or cancel the wedding. As it is, this is a sensitive area in our marriage that shouldn't exist.

Shana: Here is a problem that most people do not think of discussing. What do you do when your little six-year-old girl becomes scared, begins to cry, and wants to sleep with you?

For most parents this would not be a problem, but the newly married may resent this little person intruding in your private world of snuggling and cuddling.

(Note: My sister encountered this problem when her young stepson came on his weekend visits. She did not allow him to come into their bed. Either she or my brother-in-law would take Chris back to his bed, pray with him, and then stay with him until he was unafraid or he fell asleep. They worked together to solve the problem. It is important not to overreact to a situation like this. It may be a one-time incident or a bid for attention. Time and patience will solve many such problems.)

Marge: Ask each other about the small things. What about vacation time? Do you take the children or leave them with a grandparent? Are you thinking that this is a chance for a second honeymoon while your husband is anticipating a good time with Daddy, Mommy, and children doing family things?

Karla: After marriage I found it difficult to adjust to our lack of privacy as a couple. The children were always around. Steve allowed them to come and go in our room, take naps with us, get in bed with us at night to visit or read, and to do whatever whenever they wanted. It was hard for us to focus on each other. If we had a disagreement, the children felt protective of their father and would turn on me. It would have been better if we had been able to disagree privately. And we should have made our bedroom our private place. It could have been the one place in the house we were alone to show affection, be intimate, or even disagree if necessary. Children can be taught to respect this kind of privacy without feeling rejected.

Laurie: In Pete's first marriage, when Kay left him she wiped out his savings and their bank account. Because of this, when Pete and I got married I was not allowed to have anything to do with the checkbook.

It took years for trust to develop and for him to feel free to let me be a part of our financial planning. I felt like celebrating the strength of his trust when he consented to having my name put on the checking account.

Peter never told me what happened in his first marriage, and before we married I assumed I would have free access to any of the financial matters. Pete had decided to protect himself by not allowing access to the money. If we had just discussed this matter before we married, it would have saved a lot of hurt.

These are just a few examples of what can happen when you fail to discuss plans for your marriage. Important areas in your life are too critical to leave to assumption. Make sure of them!

Miscommunication or no communication often results in hurt turned to bitterness. You will have to conquer bitterness every time the area in which you were hurt is mentioned.

It doesn't matter how reasonable or logical your husband is, that doesn't help when you are dealing with a major disappointment or hurt. The best policy is to prevent unnecessary hurts through clear communication ahead of time.

The Reward of Honest Communication

Gayle: The first time I went to my fiance's home, I instantly noticed the television set. I knew he had one, but I was raised in a home that believed TV was wrong; therefore, we never had one in our home. Anyway, I had been around a television enough to know that I did not want to live with one. There was nothing on the screen that said, "I'm a Christian." All I had seen said quite the opposite. So a television was a big thing to me. I also noticed that he turned it on before we hardly had time to sit down. He never asked me if I minded, or what I'd like to watch. My antennas went up.

A short time later, I confronted him about it. He did not think it was wrong, and I got the feeling that the subject was closed. However, I wasn't about to let it drop so easily. I went home one night and wrote a letter. In the letter I explained my feelings about television and gave him Scripture to back up my beliefs. In closing, I said that I never intended to marry a man who had a television in his home, and that still stood true. If he was willing to dispose of it, I was willing to consider marrying him.

Yes, I was very blunt and to the point. I was not concerned about the outcome. I did not love him enough to sacrifice a strong conviction I'd carried all my life. There would be another man, another time. Better now than later, I thought.

It wasn't long before his letter arrived. Love had won out; the TV had been sold. He went on to say he had no problem choosing me over the tube and that he'd do it again in a minute! What a victory! But it would probably never have happened had I waited until after the marriage. I have kept that letter through the years and have had to show it to him on several occasions. I thank God for giving me sense enough to stand up for what I believed was right and to be willing to take the consequences.

You have everything to gain by communicating, or everything to lose if you don't!

Questions for Discussion
Here is a list of questions to help the discussion process. These questions are only the beginning. Individual needs and unique situations make it impossible to list every topic or area for planning and decision making, but you can start with this list and expand.

1. Where will we live?

2. Will we both work? Will I be a full-time mother and housewife?

3. Will we have a child together? How long will we wait? How many do we want to have?

4. How do you feel that children should be disciplined? What is my role when it comes to disciplining the children by your first marriage? What training do you feel is vital in the rearing of a child? What are the standard house rules? (For further discussion of these points see chapters 5-8.)

5. Where will we attend church? Are we spiritually compatible? Do we believe the same basic doctrine and have the same experience of salvation? Will we present a united front in these matters to our children and to ensure unity between ourselves throughout our married life? Do we agree about church attendance, tithing, and service to our church? Do we share the same spiritual goals? What are those goals?

6. In-laws and family members are important, but how much of an impact will they have on our life? How often will we visit? Is it mandatory that we spend every Sunday having dinner with your mother? In-laws from the previous marriage have a part in our lives; let's discuss in detail how big a part of our lives they will be. (See chapter 9.)

7. What are your family traditions? How do you spend your holidays? Are you willing to compromise? If so, what holidays are you willing to change in order to share my traditions with me?

8. What is the state of our finances? How do you feel about using credit cards? Where do savings and retirement funds fit into our budget? How much medical and life insurance coverage will we have? Who will pay the

bills? Who is responsible for setting the budget and controlling the finances?

9. What about friendships from the past? Do we want to associate less and less with past friends and try to seek out and build new friendships with people who have no association with your past marriage? (Note: True friends are very valuable and hard to replace. Be very cautious about discarding them.)

10. What concerns do you have about this marriage? What areas do you feel are more critical than others in making sure that we have realistic expectations of each other?

11. What do you want in marriage and as a family?

12. What are our strengths and what are our weaknesses?

Ask these questions and ask them again. See if the verbal response stands the test of time.

It Is Never Too Late!

If you are already married you probably can give a few of your own examples of what happens when you don't discuss the issues before marriage. But please don't say, "It's too late!" Maybe something in this chapter can help you deal with your own disappointments or frustrations. If there are unresolved situations in your marriage, sit down with your spouse and go through the questions for discussion. Try to find short- and long-term solutions for your problems.

In discussing each question ask yourself the following questions:

• How are things now?

- How do I want them to be?
- What can I do to put my desires in action?
- What are my personal short-term and long-term goals?
- What are our short-term and long-term goals as a couple?
- What areas can I compromise in? List them.
- What areas in our marriage am I willing to accept as is? (I realize that change in these areas would be very difficult.)

The Foundation of a Successful Marriage

Marriage

first means the union of two
who love one another through
and through. But as the years
go by, it's easier to see
we need the Lord
too. A good
marriage takes
three.
—Anonymous

*W*ithout God our marriage will always lack an extra-special quality. We must put Him first as the builder of our home, make Him the first priority in our hectic schedule, and allow Him to be our instructor in life's love lessons.

This chapter will look at God's purpose in marriage, the biblical roles of husband and wife, and several essential ingredients for a successful marriage.

A Partnership Based on Committed Love

All of us desire to have someone for our very own. Someone who will care for us and about us. Someone who is willing to share with us and sacrifice for us. A special someone to lean on in hard times and celebrate with in the good times. With a best friend you can break down the barriers of your real self and have no fear of rejection, but just receive loving acceptance. A best friend for life.

When I lived and worked in Athens, Greece, under the Associates In Missions program, I had a best friend. I went to that country knowing no one and came away having one of the best friends a person could have, Ellen. We could be ourselves with each other; we encouraged each other to reach our full potential; we had the same goals as single women involved in missions; we shared high joys and deep disappointments; and she never expected me to do her wash or have dinner ready when she came in from work! We were on cloud nine and would have been content to spend the remainder of our lives in Greece as single women missionaries.

But after a time I discovered the difference between a best friend and a marriage partner. That difference is commitment.

Best friends can share the same goals, but still each

lives his or her life to the best interests of self. That fact doesn't take away from the friendship. For friends to pledge their lives to each other would be abnormal. But marriage partners are best friends who are committed to the best interests of each other. When I married my husband I went a step further than any other friendship. I have a best friend who is committed to me for life.

Ellen and I have gone our separate ways. She is working in Papua, New Guinea, and I am married and in New Jersey. We still love each other and pray for each other, we still stay in touch, and we still encourage each other. I am interested in her activities and goals, as she is in mine. Our friendship is good, but it reached its limits. With my husband there are no limits outside of the ones we put on the relationship.

The purpose of marriage is more than to satisfy physical desire. Marriage is a lifelong commitment of love. That love will grow stronger, and the desire to love and show affection to each other will grow with it.

By contrast, lust will not stand the test of time and hardships. Lust is a weed, but love is a flower.

Nine days before Stan and I married I received a letter from him, which said, "I love you, Cindy. I want more than anything for us to always be happy together. It seems there are so many marriages where couples can't even be friends anymore. There is no respect for each other's feelings. I pray God will always help me to be loving and understanding."

A successful marriage is built on respect for each other and true friendship. Without these a marriage will not survive.

Role of the Husband

The Bible commands husbands to love their wives. Not just to love, but to love them as Christ loved the church and gave Himself for it. "Husbands, love your wives, even as Christ also loved the church, and gave himself for it. . . . So ought men to love their wives as their own bodies. He that loveth his wife loveth himself" (Ephesians 5:25, 28).

I Corinthians 13:4-8 describes true, godly love, the kind that husbands and wives need to have for each other, the kind that will make a tremendous difference in a marriage.

Charity suffereth long, and is kind; charity envieth not; charity vaunteth not itself, is not puffed up, doth not behave itself unseemly, seeketh not her own, is not easily provoked, thinketh no evil; rejoiceth not in iniquity, but rejoiceth in the truth; beareth all things, believeth all things, hopeth all things, endureth all things. Charity never faileth.

Here is my paraphrase of this passage: Love is patient; love is kind. Love does not envy when someone else has success or receives attention. Love does not cause bragging or boasting of self; it does not swell with pride or importance, does not behave in an unbecoming manner, does not go after self-gain, is not easy to be provoked, does not think negative or destructive thoughts, and does not have a mind full of wickedness. Love does not exult in injustice, but exults in honesty and sincerity. Love tolerates all things, and has confidence in all things, desires and expects all things, has strength to bear all things. Love never gives up nor lets you down.

The husband is to cherish and honor his wife. "Likewise, ye husbands, dwell with them according to knowledge, giving honour unto the wife, as unto the weaker vessel, and as being heirs together of the grace of life; that your prayers be not hindered" (I Peter 3:7).

The husband has the responsibility to provide for the family. "But if any provide not for his own, and specially for those of his own house, he hath denied the faith, and is worse than an infidel" (I Timothy 5:8).

Role of the Wife

The Bible commands the wife to respect her husband. "And the wife see that she reverence her husband" (Ephesians 5:33).

It is easy to submit to someone you respect. A wife should not focus on her husband's flaws but instead recognize her own. Instead of constantly trying to improve her husband, she should try to improve herself. The Bible tells her to respect and submit to his leadership role in the marriage partnership. "Wives, submit yourselves unto your own husbands, as unto the Lord" (Ephesians 5:22).

According to Genesis 2:18, "And the LORD God said, It is not good that the man should be alone; I will make him an help meet for him." He created the woman as a helper or aid suitable for the man. A wife is not merely a companion for her husband; she is also the complement to her husband. She is able to meet his physical and emotional needs.

A survey found that the qualities men value in a wife are as follows:
- Being a friend.
- Being a good listener. Many men said that their wives talked too much and didn't listen enough.
- Advising without lecturing.
- Correcting without shaming.
- Being a positive thinker.
- Feeding their self-confidence and fueling their enthusiasm.
- Being a confidant, allowing the husband to expose his hurts and hopes in complete confidence.
- Being a homemaker—creator of "home." (See chapter 8.)
- Sexual fulfillment.

Titus 2:3-5 tells the older women, those with experience, to teach the following to younger women:
- Be sober (serious or calm)
- Love your husband
- Love your children
- Be discreet
- Be chaste
- Be keepers at home
- Be good
- Be obedient (respectful and cooperative) to your own husband

Christian women should live in this manner so that the Word of God is not blasphemed (Titus 2:5).

Ingredients for a Successful Marriage
Successful marriages have several key ingredients:

- commitment
- love
- acceptance
- understanding
- communication
- appreciation
- sexual fulfillment
- romance
- support
- balance
- recreation

What happens when moonlight and roses turn to daylight and dishes? When reality of everyday living comes home to you, will you be prepared for it? The answer lies in these ingredients. Let us look at them briefly.

Commitment

As the earth orbits around the sun and depends on it to sustain life, so marriage revolves around commitment. A marriage will be no stronger than the partners' desire to fulfill their promise of "for better or for worse, in sickness and in health, for richer or for poorer . . .till death do us part." As we have already discussed, the essence of marriage is commitment.

Love

We must not confuse love with infatuation. Infatuation is an ardent temporary affection, but true love is consistent and lasting. As we have already discussed the Bible teaches husbands and wives to love each other, and I Corinthians 13 presents the ideal of love.

Acceptance

Perhaps you wanted a millionaire and married a working man. Perhaps you wanted a preacher and married a policeman. If you love the man for himself and don't try to change him, that is acceptance. Acceptance is saying, "I love you just the way you are."

Understanding

When there are arguments or disagreements, here are a few rules for maintaining or restoring peace in your home.

1. *Be willing to apologize.* If you aren't sorry for your views or for what you said, you can be sorry for hurting your spouse's feelings or for contributing to tension in the home.

2. *Maintain stability.* After you disagree don't brood or sulk. Keep a good attitude and get things back to normal as quickly as possible.

3. *Submit yourself through prayer.* Pray for your attitude to be right, forgive so that you can receive forgiveness for your wrong, and allow the Lord to cleanse resentment and frustration out of your life. After you have been cleansed, forgiven, and renewed through prayer, it is much easier to be the wife you need to be.

I learned a lesson one day after a disagreement with my husband. It was an argument we had had before, with the same responses and the same hurt on both of our parts. I prayed, "Lord, I don't want this experience to be in vain. Let me learn something from this."

As I lay on the sofa thinking over what had happened earlier, I realized that I looked to my husband for protection, encouragement, and total fulfillment. I needed to turn to God and look to Him for strength, and then I would have the confidence that only comes through the Spirit. God can give us self-confidence, joy, strength, and security. We must be careful of the demands we put on our husbands. Our spouse can only meet a limited amount of our needs, but God can meet all of our needs. By going to God in prayer and allowing Him to work, we can avoid putting a bigger load than necessary on our beloved.

Communication

Communication is vital in marriage. Here are some guidelines in this area.

1. *Learn to express your thoughts and ideas.*

2. *Be a patient listener.* Do not try to put words in your partner's mouth in order to speed a conversation along.

3. *Pay attention.* Do not be so busy readying your reply and looking for the first opportunity to interrupt that valuable feelings and ideas slip past unheeded. "In the multitude of words there wanteth not sin: but he that refraineth his lips is wise" (Proverbs 10:19).

4. *Know what kind of communicator your spouse is.* I am detail oriented, while my husband likes to get to the meat of the matter. Do not be frustrated if you are opposites. Be willing to work together. The detail-oriented communicator should be willing to identify the problem first and then go on with condensed details. The facts-only—please communicator should be willing to elaborate with a few details.

5. *Do not be rude.* For example, if your mate shares

something that is serious to him but humorous to you, don't embarrass him by laughing or making a joke out of the matter.

6. *Do not act impatient or bored* with your spouse when he is trying to talk to you.

7. *Show you are listening by asking questions or summarizing what has been said:* "How did you feel when that happened?" "What you are saying is . . ." "What happened to make you feel this way?" "Give me examples."

8. *Do not attack your partner verbally* because you feel defensive or because you don't like what you are hearing. Give him time to explain himself. "He that answereth a matter before he heareth it, it is a folly and shame unto him" (Proverbs 18:13).

9. *Be honest and open.* Do not let pride stand in the way of a closer relationship. "Speaking the truth in love . . ." (Ephesians 4:15).

10. *Do not ignore your mate* because you feel unable to cope with his problems or unable to help him find a solution to his problem. If your husband shares something with you, be loving enough to acknowledge that you heard him and that you feel unable to help him find the solution.

Here are some additional scriptural teachings on communication:

• *A man hath joy by the answer of his mouth: and a word spoken in due season, how good is it!* (Proverbs 15:23).

• *A word fitly spoken is like apples of gold in pictures of silver* (Proverbs 25:11).

- *A wholesome tongue is a tree of life* (Proverbs 15:4).
- *Let all bitterness, and wrath, and anger, and clamour, and evil speaking, be put away from you, with all malice* (Ephesians 4:31).

Appreciation

Appreciation is to marriage as water is to a thirsty man. Just a few well-timed words can make the hardest task easier. The phrase "I appreciate you for . . ." will make a rainy day full of sunshine. When someone you love notices and values your efforts, it makes all your work worthwhile. Praise and appreciation motivate you to do more.

Check your vocabulary. Do these phrases appear often?

- Thank you
- I appreciate you
- You are sweet
- You are a good husband to me
- I love you because you are a good provider
- I value your thoughts and opinions

Sexual Fulfillment

Proverbs 5:18-19 instructs, "Rejoice with the wife of thy youth. Let her be as the loving hind and pleasant roe; let her breasts satisfy thee at all times; and be thou ravished [enraptured, transported with joy] always with her love."

In order for a husband to be enraptured with his wife's love she must be willing to give him love. Withholding love or affection or physical attention from your spouse because of an argument, or as a punishment for not getting your own way, is wrong. (See I Corinthians 7:3-5.) Those who do so hurt themselves.

At times perhaps there isn't anything specifically wrong, but you are just out of sorts. Take time to be alone and love each other, to become one flesh. Doing so will help maintain harmony in your marriage and bring peace between you and your mate.

Deal maturely with any problems you have. Be sensitive to your spouse's needs and desires. Don't be as the small child who pouts, "If you don't play what I want to play, then I'm going home." Allow your spouse to be transported with joy and enraptured with your love.

Romance

Dayle: Everyone wants a romantic marriage, and I'm no exception. But let's face it, a lot of things about being married are just *not* romantic: washing dirty underwear, cleaning dirty ovens, dishpan hands, paying bills, spanking kids, and the list goes on and on. Even so, we should strive to have a certain amount of romance in our marriage. How to do this depends largely on what type person you are, and how bad you want it.

Romance comes easily during courtship. You couldn't wait until Friday night when you would see that charming, handsome prince of yours, and you longed for how he looked, how he smelled, how he talked, and how he looked at you. Ah yes, Friday night is going to be great you thought! And it usually was.

The same principles hold true if you're going to have

a romantic marriage. You must feel romantic. You must think romantic thoughts. That can be difficult at times. A marriage cannot be constantly romantic, for life is not a fantasy land of white lace and promises, candlelights and roses. There are unromantic things about being married. Still, you should try to find romantic times as often as possible.

An important part of romance is setting the mood. Romance doesn't thrive when you eat a meal of canned spaghetti on a paper plate. It can develop if you sincerely want it to, but it's harder if the setting is improper. If you have children, it gets harder and harder to set the mood for romance. It may be easier to get a sitter and go out than to create a romantic mood at home.

But if you want to set the mood in your own home, prepare your evening meal far enough in advance to give yourself some spare time before your husband comes home. It may mean cooking the night before.

In those few hours or minutes before your spouse arrives home, take some time to freshen up, take your bath and put on something pleasant to look at. Fix your hair, and dab a little perfume here and there.

When he arrives, be attentive. Offer to get him something to drink or run his bath water. Ask him when he wants dinner. Above all, listen! Try to absorb every word he says and find out how his day went. Don't interrupt him while he is talking—unless it's to tell him how dashingly handsome he looks.

The most important ingredient in achieving a romantic marriage is learning how to give. If you're always concerned about being on the receiving end, you'll probably wind up being miserable and depressed because you feel slighted.

Romance is part of a balanced, happy marriage but it is not realistic to expect twenty-four hours of romance day after day.

Be happy with the little things. Does he have to bring a dozen roses home, or will the rose he cuts off the bush in the front yard count?

Romance is putting thoughtfulness in your marriage.

Support

My husband knows that I am the president of his fan club. I am for him one hundred percent. I may not always like his decisions, but I love him and respect him; therefore, I support him. How?

- When he is discouraged I will encourage him.
- When he is sick I will nurse him.
- When he has an idea I will not say, "It won't work," but I will say, "What can we do to make it work?"
- When he is struggling with a problem I will be strong and pray for him.
- I will be his cheerful assistant in his endeavors.
- I will verbalize my belief in him and his efforts.

Balance

Balance is a matter of keeping priorities in the right order. A couple should not become so absorbed with each other that they exclude the children. They should not get so far into debt that they hold two jobs to pay the creditors. They should not allow family activities or projects to cut into their time with God and their church attendance.

We must learn to balance and not to overextend ourselves by becoming deeply involved in too many areas of activity. Life brings many demands on our time, and we must learn to discipline ourselves. We should allow time for ourselves, but we shouldn't live just for ourselves. It is important to learn to say no to any outside interest that would put our time with God, husband, and children in jeopardy.

Recreation

Everyone needs diversion from the monotony of work, eat, and sleep. Your recreation should not be limited to a yearly two-week vacation. Be spontaneous! Think fun! Recreation can range from simple and inexpensive to elaborate and costly.

If you were dating what would you plan to do tonight? How long has it been since you shared a good laugh with your children?

Have a picnic. If the weather doesn't permit a trip to a park, you can do what Ellen and I did when we lived in Greece. After days of pouring cold rain we moved our furniture back, spread blankets on the floor, pulled the heater as close as possible, lit some candles (it was night), and pigged out! Use your imagination!

Why Do I Love?

I love you
    not only for what you are
    but for what I am when I am with you.
I love you
    not only for what you have made of yourself
    but for what you are making of me.

I love you
> for ignoring the possibilities of the fool in me and for laying hold on the possibilities of the good in me.

I love you
> because you are helping me to make of the lumber in my life, not a tavern, but a temple, and of the words of my every day, not a reproach, but a song.

I love you
> because your very presence makes me happy. Without a word, without a touch, without a sign, our love is there. You have won my love by just being yourself, and because you are guided by faith in God and His promises for men and women who build godly houses.

—Anonymous

♥♥♥ 4 ♥♥♥♥♥♥♥♥♥.

Keeping Your Identity

They measuring themselves by themselves, and comparing themselves among themselves, are not wise (II Corinthians 10:12).

*P*eople will compare. It is human nature to do so. We would probably do the same if we were not aware of the damage that can be done in lives because of this habit.

You are an individual. Unique. Created in the image of God but definitely your own person. Someone once remarked to me in reference to my husband's first wife, "You must find it very difficult to fill Cyndy's shoes." I answered, "I don't even try. She had areas in which she was very talented. God has put me in my new role; therefore, He must have seen abilities in me that Stan, the children, and my church needed."

We can fill a void, but we don't have to try to fill someone's shoes. It is hard walking around in shoes that don't fit.

Still it hurts to think that people feel that you don't measure up to the previous spouse. It is shocking the remarks and reactions that some people, even some Christians, can make. I've been told everything imaginable.

- "Just think, when Stan is embracing you and calls out Cyndy's name, you will never know it."
- "He is only marrying you because he needs a maid and a nanny."
- "He will never love you like he loved Cyndy, but you are a sweet girl."

The devil will bring these cruel remarks to your mind at a time when you are feeling most negative about yourself, your new role as a parent, or your new marriage. You must learn to ignore these comments and be victorious.

I can only hope that your spouse is as good at trying to understand as mine has been. Stan explained to me that his life is like a book; when the chapter with Cyndy ended, that was it, and we are a new chapter.

Even though you may want to share every thought, every hurt, and every negative comparison with your spouse, it is better not to do so. You want to share the negative comparison because you want your spouse to refute it and to insist that you are worth your weight in gold. But what if refuting the comparison would make your husband feel as if he is betraying his first wife? What if she was really more talented in a certain area than you are? Every woman wants to be the most beautiful, talented, and brilliant woman in her man's life, so your desire to shine isn't wrong, but it is wrong to put your husband in a position in which he has to compare. If you want to come out the winner, then ban comparing in your marriage; otherwise it can eventually destroy your relationship.

In writing this chapter I hesitated to share the comments that were made to me. A few of them were exceptionally rude, crude, and socially unacceptable! I did so to show that I have been in that situation. I understand the hurt and humiliation. I know what it is like to have a negative thought crop up and wonder, Could it be true?

Bring such thoughts into subjection. Discipline yourself not to allow hurtful thoughts to stay in your mind. Do not dwell on the negative, but replace that thought with a positive thought: My husband loves me. I know he does because he always makes sure I have a Diet Coke!

If you don't want your husband to compare you with his first wife, then don't put thoughts of comparing in his mind.

Comments on Being Compared

Angela: How about when your husband compares you to his ex-wife? When I was pregnant, Ralph told me that when he was married to Lisa she watched everything she ate as soon as she found out she was pregnant. Now she was a woman who could blow away with a strong wind. She couldn't gain weight if she ate twenty-four hours a day.

Keli: My in-laws were good at giving advice by using the ex-wife as an example, whether it was in my favor or not. I'm sick of stories and examples that my in-laws use to make me a better wife and mother. I hate hearing about my husband's first wife!

Jane: I lived near my husband's in-laws from his first marriage. Because of the children they were always stopping in, and it was a nightmare for me. They checked the house out to find any changes I had made, and if they saw a change that I had made they would criticize it by saying something like, "Oh, my daughter hated that color" or "My daughter would never have put the picture over there." I was uncomfortable decorating my own home and allowed them to undermine my confidence in redecorating my home.

Dave: My wife was married to a genius the first time. I'm not mechanically inclined, and even though I try, I feel rather than hear her comparing. I would almost rather that she verbalize the comparison, because it is hard to deal with her silent disapproval of my efforts. Just knowing how skilled her first husband was, together with her obviously silent frustration at my inabilities, makes me feel hurt and uncomfortable.

Shelly: No one else had to compare me with my husband's first wife. I was so busy doing that myself. There were a lot of comparisons made (never by my husband), which encouraged me in this self-destructing habit that was forming.

Lauren: When I married, my two new sons decided that their mother was the only one who could do things right. It was a constant stream of "My mom doesn't put mustard on my sandwich" and "My mom doesn't make me do my homework at the table; she lets me lay on the floor." The hardest to deal with was "Dad loved my mom more than he loves you" and "My mom is prettier and nicer than you." It was total rejection of me in every way.

Responding to Comparisons

Lauren: I had to get over the feeling of personal rejection and realize that it was natural for the boys to think more of their mom. For things like homework, housework, or personal habits of cleanliness I would reply, "Well, we do things this way at our house," and I used a non threatening, even tone.

I tried to be firm, but casual. When the comparison became personal, like "My mom is prettier than you," I would agree that their mother was very attractive and find some way to compliment her. The boys were shocked by this and soon started to say nice things in return about me. In dealing with their feelings that "Daddy loved Mommy better," I would just say, "People love each other in different ways. Your daddy loved your mommy when they were married, but now Daddy and I are married and he loves me. It doesn't mean he loved either one of us better." I didn't try to ignore their statements or argue with them, but I tried to make them feel good about my answers.

Dayle: It took a while for the realization to sink in that I was the only newlywed in our relationship. My husband had seven years of experience at being married. He was not, and could not be, a newlywed. This was very difficult for me. I had been very close to my family before my marriage, so naturally I missed them very much. He, on the other hand, had been away from home for ten years. He had a hard time relating to my homesickness at times. I think he also expected a lot more of me than a man who had never been married would have. A man who has been married for quite a few years doesn't expect his wife to burn the beans. He doesn't expect her to forget his mother's birthday. But the woman who is marrying for the first time has much to learn that only comes from experience. If the husband is not careful, he will forget that she is new at living together and sharing all her time, money, energy, and love with one human being for twenty-four hours a day.

Before I married my husband, my dear mother-in-law and sister-in-law to be went over to my husband's home, scoured, cleaned, and put away some old memories, trying to make way for a new family member. This helped greatly, but I still could see "her" signature on everything around me.

I was fortunate to have a wonderful, generous church shower and received many nice gifts (such as towels, sheets, wall hangings, dishes, clocks, and lamps). But I often had a sense that I didn't belong in my new home. In time, I redecorated, recarpeted, repainted, and learned to love the place. I cried the day we moved. My baby had been born there; many happy, as well as sad, memories were made in that home.

If you're like we were, most newlyweds can't afford to totally refurbish the place, so you have to make the best of it. Buy some throw rugs, get a couch cover, make new drapes from sheets, paint the walls. Lots of little things can make a place look and feel like your own. I would stress that worrying over things you cannot change will only make you very unhappy. Concentrate on the more positive side of using "her" things. Our first Christmas, I found some old Christmas decorations that the family had used in their past Christmases. They were very pretty, and I enjoyed hanging them around the house. I was just grateful I didn't have to buy a lot of unnecessary things. Believe it or not, I still have some of those things and still use them. They do not bother me in the least.

While keeping your identity can be tough, it is possible.

Healthy Self-Esteem

There are two definitions for the word *pride*. It can mean arrogance or conceit, or it can be used to refer to self-respect. Proverbs 16:18 says, "Pride goeth before destruction, and an haughty spirit before a fall." Obviously, this verse speaks of arrogance and reveals that it is destructive. But there is a difference between a healthy ego and an unhealthy pride.

A proper sense of self-esteem is essential to a happy life. If you are secure in yourself and if you have self-respect, the barbed comments or negative comparisons from others will not hurt nearly as badly. Those who battle poor self-image more than arrogance and conceit need to learn to improve their attitude regarding themselves.

We learn in the Word of God that as members of a spiritual body we are all important though our spiritual gifts are different. It is the same with our natural gifts and talents. You will be amazed at the joy and confidence that will come into your life when you begin to discover your talents and abilities.

Each person has her own areas that she will excel in. Develop your talents and build your confidence at the same time.

You were created in the image of God. He gave you talents and abilities. Be yourself, not a carbon copy of someone else. Shake off feelings of inadequacy and discover the real you.

At a New Jersey/Delaware District ladies retreat, Sister Janet Trout shared some steps on building a proper sense of self-esteem:

1. Be kind to everyone (Galatians 6:10).
2. Do your best in all situations.
3. Desiring is not the same as doing your best.
4. Do not give yourself negative labels.
5. When you fail, admit it but refuse to condemn self.
6. Improve your behavior, and self-esteem will improve.
7. Do not compare self to others.
8. Concentrate on God's grace and acceptance.
9. Associate with friends who are true friends.
10. Choose friends as carefully as you would choose a house to live in.
11. Start helping other people by seeing them as God sees them.
12. Learn to laugh.
13. Have expectations that are realistic.

♥.♥.♥.♥. 5 .♥.♥.♥.♥.♥.♥.♥.♥.

Mother: More Than a Title

Instant motherhood is not easy—not for the new mother nor the family she is so eagerly trying to mother. Time is the greatest gift God ever gave the new mom.

I read of a woman who wanted to open a home for bewildered mothers. The first few months of motherhood would have qualified me for acceptance in such a place.

Labor pains do not make a woman a true mother. It is the labors of love—caring, nurturing, and listening—that qualify her to be a mother. A woman becomes a real mother by loving and nurturing her child. Titles do not matter. It is the relationship she develops with the child that counts.

A mother is a teacher, someone who trains and instructs. Proverbs 22:6 says, "Train up a child in the way he should go: and when he is old, he will not depart from it." Mothers are in the business of training. The word *train* means, according to *Webster's New College* dictionary, to form by instruction and discipline; to teach so as to make fit, qualified, or proficient; to make prepared for a test of skill. If we as mothers do our jobs right, when life's tests come to our children, they will be prepared. They will be able to come through the test victorious.

The following poem by an unknown author expresses the importance of the mother's teaching role.

Two Temples

A builder builded a temple;
   He wrought with care and skill:
Pillars and groins and arches
   Were fashioned to meet his will.
And men said when they saw its beauty:
   "It shall never know decay.
Great is thy skill, O builder,
   Thy fame shall endure for aye."

A teacher builded a temple;
   She wrought with skill and care:
Forming each pillar with patience,
   Laying each stone with prayer.
None saw the unceasing effort;
   None knew of the marvelous plan;
For the temple the teacher builded
   Was unseen by the eyes of man.

Gone is the builder's temple,
   Crumbled into dust;
Pillar and groin and arches
   Food for consuming rust.

> But the temple the teacher builded
> Shall endure while the ages roll;
> For that beautiful, unseen temple
> Was a child's immortal soul.
> —Anonymous

Most stepparents start out trying to be the perfect parent and settle for being a good parent. All parents go through school with their children, a school they will never graduate from. Each age level is a different grade. Each child is a separate subject to be studied.

Society has given us images of the perfect mother, saying, If you really love your child you will be like this or you will behave a certain way. These are images most of us will find impossible to live up to, and then we must deal with guilt and condemnation over our lack of love for our child. The only standard we should be concerned about living up to is the standard that God has set for us. We don't need to feel guilty for being human. Let us try to be the best parent we can and trust in the Lord.

Mothering is work! It requires commitment, unselfishness, and consistency.

You must be confident in yourself as a mother. Without confidence you will be an easy victim for parental peer pressure: "But all the other mothers are letting their children go . . ."

Yes, mothering is work, but the rewards are many. Being loved and respected by your child is worth all your parental efforts. Your children will bring you laughter, and their accomplishments will cause your heart to swell with thanksgiving. At night when you tuck your little fresh-bathed, sleepy-eyed darling into bed and she wraps her fat, little, dimpled arms around you and squeezes as hard as she can while whispering, "I love you, Mommy," or when your sweaty, dirty little boy comes trailing mud through your freshly mopped kitchen wearing a smile as big as Texas and as radiant as the sunshine outside because he is bringing his mommy flowers that he went out in the field to pick—well, it is times like these that make you say, "Thank you, God, for giving me children."

Advice for Parents

• *Be consistent.* Children need and want to know what is expected of them. Be consistent in your discipline, house rules, and lifestyle.

• *Be available.* You must give one-hundred-percent loyalty to your family in order to receive one-hundred-percent loyalty in return. Give your children top priority. Be there when they need you.

• *Provide security, acceptance, and approval.* Parents have a responsibility to let their children know, "God gave you to me, and I want you in my life."

• *Teach them goal planning.* Children need to be challenged with goals beyond their reach. Everyone wants to be productive, and children are no exception.

• *Establish regular procedures.* They bring security. Children do not like sudden changes. They want to feel that they are involved in bringing about the changes in their lives.

• *Compliment your child.* We are all sensitive to criticism and to negative feelings or thoughts. Children are more so. It seems they have a sixth sense for detecting negative feelings toward them. For every negative comment about your child it takes four positive comments to restore a good feeling about himself.

• *Have a close relationship with your child.* Listen to your child and value his opinions.

• *Teach decision making.* Teach your child to look for the pro and the con in every situation.

• *Choose your battles carefully.* Don't make everything an issue. If you are flexible over things of little or no consequence, your child will be more open and willing to listen to instruction and laws in important areas.

• *Share your world with your children.* I enjoy crafts, and even though there are times when it is much easier to work alone, I find a way to include my children, April and Jonathan, in my projects. Find a hobby that you can enjoy together. You can learn much about your child through conversation as you work together.

• *Mealtimes are important.* Since breakfast is the only meal before you part, try to keep it sweet. Share wishes and hopes for the day. Give encouragement. Since the dinner hour is a coming together after the daylong separation, welcome conversation from each member of the family. Make it a pleasant, happy time.

• *Know your children's friends.* Let your home be a refuge for them and their friends. My parents had more teenagers in their home than they would have ever thought possible. Many times my sister and I would come home to find a friend already there spending time with our parents. Some of the girls found it much easier to talk with my mother and get advice, and some of our "boyfriends" found in my father a better friend, encourager, and instructor than their natural father.

• *Avoid criticizing your child's friends.* Out of loyalty to the friendship they will defend the friend. Why make a battleground? You can point out things in a friendship that may bother you, but try not to make an open attack.

My parents had a lot of wisdom in dealing with teenage friendships. They made their home and lives open to all of our friends. They figured as long as we were home and involved with them they could control what was happening. My father would be in the back yard manning the grill with the help of a few guys on nice weekends. My mother was the first to volunteer our home for a church youth party or welcome warmly the ones who just dropped in to visit or spend the night. Our friends knew that there was room to come and be a part of a family anytime at our house. My girlfriends knew that when they stayed over at our house there would be a curfew and rules, and everyone knew that my mom would be waiting up to talk over a snack or pray because of a hurt or disappointment.

The curfews and rules did not keep our friends away. They did not grumble and complain about them because it was fun at my house. There was love, warmth, acceptance, comfort, and security at my house. Why? Because of two parents who cared not only about their teenagers, but their teenager's friends too!

• *Know the parents of your child's friend.* We have a rule that our children cannot visit the home of someone if we do not know the parents.

• *Get to know your child's teachers.* Meet them on the first day of school. Let them know you are a concerned parent ready to be involved in the school year.

• *Set limits for your children.* Show them that the guidelines and rules come from concern for them and not because you don't trust them. April has begged to walk to school, but she would have to cross a very busy street and go a short distance through a wooded area. I don't allow it because I want to protect my daughter from even a chance of her being kidnapped, but not wanting to create fear in her, I initially did not give her a reason. April took this to mean that I didn't trust her. She took every opportunity to impress me with how trustworthy she was. Finally I explained why I didn't allow her to walk to school, gave her examples of children who had been taken and never returned, and repeatedly assured her, "I trust you; it is the sick people who steal children that I don't trust." At that point she accepted this rule without complaint.

My mother had a firm rule that carried grave consequences if broken: "If you are going to be late, call home and inform me." Even as an adult living at home, I always called my mom if I knew I was going to be later than I had said. My parents usually knew where they could find me at any given time.

• *Give your child accurate information on the facts of life.* Don't let schools, friends, or strangers teach your children about sex, drugs, substance abuse, dating, puberty, or any other topic that is personal and is the responsibility of the mother and father. As a new parent, don't assume what your new children have been taught. Find out what they know and decide with your spouse when and how each subject will be discussed. If the child approaches you with questions, deal with them at that moment. Don't be embarrassed or give evasive answers.

Explanations on these matters are part of your job of training your child.

A young cousin took it upon herself to explain the facts of life to April when she was still rather young, and the explanation left her confused. I began to realize this and decided we needed a private talk. One Sunday afternoon April and I went early to the church, stopping to get a soda on the way. Our church has lovely grounds, and the day was warm and sunshiny. We talked and I slowly brought the subject around. Even though she was embarrassed at first, we had a good talk, and she was able to get accurate answers to her questions. Now April knows she can come to me about every question and I am ready and willing to talk with her.

When I was pregnant with Nathan, I had plenty of opportunity to have talks with Jonathan on how babies are formed in the mother and the way God made for babies to be born. I kept the discussion simple and on his seven-year-old level, but he was informed.

I want open communication with my sons as well as my daughter. Our home, Mommy and Daddy, is their resource. We need to be available with love and answers for them.

Be prepared to explain why you live the way you do. If your child asks why it is wrong to drink alcohol, your answer will make a better impact if you can give a biblical answer and follow it up with examples of the evils that alcohol causes.

• *Pray with your children.* Your children will learn to pray by listening to you. Pray for them before they leave for school. Pray over meals and show them thankfulness. Pray for the special needs in their lives, such as an important test at school, trouble with a friend, or sickness.

• *Start the morning off with a verse of Scripture.* The Word of God is anointed. Our favorite morning verse is Psalm 118:24: "This is the day which the LORD hath made; we will rejoice and be glad in it." If a family member is having a bad day, I quote this verse and emphasize, "We will rejoice and be glad in it." Soon the day is going better. A smile appears, and once again God's anointed Word has ministered and been uplifting.

Another favorite verse that I like for the children to quote before they leave for school is Psalm 19:14: "Let the words of my mouth, and the meditation of my heart, be acceptable in thy sight, O LORD, my strength, and my redeemer." After April and Jonathan quote the verse, I ask one of them to define the "words of my mouth and meditation of my heart." Without hestiation the answer comes back, "Words that I say and thoughts that I think." Make sure your child understands what the Scripture is saying.

• *Give your children responsibilities.* Children enjoy being part of a team. Children should know that every member of the family must work together. Give your children responsibilities according to their age and capabilities. We developed a star-chart system for our home. Each child had a star chart with the days of the week listed across the top and the jobs he or she was responsible for listed down the side. Each day the task was completed a colored star was put in the appropriate box. If the child did an exceptional job then two stars were put up instead of one. This system gave the children incentive to fill their chart with stars and thereby get their work done. Both children and parents were very pleased.

• *Get involved in your children's school.* Most teachers appreciate parental involvement. Join the P.T.A. Perhaps you can become a room mother. Ask the teacher if you can celebrate your child's birthday by sending cupcakes and juice. (Remember also to send the napkins and cups.) Send a snack for your child to share with the class. Volunteer to help with a class field trip. Attend class parties and take pictures for your child's memory book.

• *Take your children to the local library.* Get them a card and teach them to be responsible for their books. When April "lost" a book in her room we had her pay the fine. She was more careful after that. Look through the books your child chooses to make sure it is a good, clean book. One day I picked up a book April had brought home from the library. As I scanned the pages, I was shocked to see curse words and immoral thoughts in a book written for twelve-year-olds. From that day on I read every book that my children bring home. Since I have pointed out to the children what I want and expect in the books that they bring home, I have rarely found a book that didn't meet my standards. In fact, April is quick to close a book she is reading and put it in the stack of books going back to the library if she comes across something she thinks I would object to.

• *Spend time with your children.* Read to your children. Play games with them. Laugh with them. Help them with homework. Listen to their dreams.

• *Be affectionate.* Give hugs and kisses as often as possible.

• *Allow your child time alone with your husband.* Don't be jealous of time your husband spends with his child. Encourage a good relationship between father and child.

The Wicked Stepmother: Disciplining Your Child

The biggest issue in a second marriage is discipline of the children by the stepparent. The group discussion at a marriage retreat will bear out this fact. Consider these common observations.

• The stepparent doesn't understand my child.
• The stepparent is being unfair.
• If the couple has a child together, automatically the stepparent is partial to "their" child.

I wish that I could dispute every one of the foregoing comments, but the sad part of our story is that sometimes they are true. There are stepparents who do not love, try to understand, discipline in fairness, or behave equally in dealing with "our" and "his" children. On the other hand, there are natural parents who are guilty of the same behavior. In defense of the stepmother, let me present the following responses.

• *Time brings understanding.* If you are in a family long enough you will get to know the child. Actually, the stepparent may see the child in a more accurate light than a parent who is so blinded with a spirit of "I must protect my baby from everyone including the mother of the home." If you raise a child to believe that he has suffered and therefore the world owes him a recompense, the child will have a hard adjustment in the real world of adulthood.

Basically, the world couldn't care less what an adult suffered as a child. An employer will not overlook a poor work record because the employee lost his mother at the age of five. A university will not pass a failing student because her parents divorced when she was a baby and she never knew her father. Instead of judging a stepparent for lack of understanding, the other parent should try to see the child in a new light. With the "real" parent's understanding of the child and the insight of the new parent, a balance can be worked out in the child's best interest.

• *The only solution is for the parents to sit down together and establish house rules.* The method of discipline, the severity of it, and who will administer it must be decided. When the parents are in total agreement, they should call the children in and explain these rules and the results if the rules are broken. Then be prepared to be tested. Children will try you to see if you mean what you say!

• *Sibling rivalry is as old as Cain and Abel.* One obvious fact about children who have been added to a family is that they are younger than the others. Younger children in any family situation, natural or bonded, are picked on or excluded by their brothers and sisters. Parents must look out for the youngest child. Does that automatically make the stepmother partial?

• *Every person is different.* What really annoys you may be considered frivolous by someone else. Get to the root of the problem. Does the excessive silliness bother you, or is it the attention the child gets from such behavior that bothers you?

• *Be reasonable in your expectations.* Be honest with yourself and your spouse. Learn to relax. Is the problem as bad as you think, or are you overreacting? You cannot expect a child who has been brought up one way to adjust easily and quickly to a different behavior or lifestyle.

In a group discussion on stepparenting the question was asked, "Should the stepparent be allowed to discipline without the natural parent stepping in?" A lively discussion followed. Here are the highlights.

Karl: What's sauce for the goose is sauce for the gander. If one party is truly being harder on the stepkids than the other children, well, then there is going to be friction. If the rule is a rule and Johnny gets a spanking for eating ice cream before dinner, then Susie gets a spanking too. The treatment needs to be equal. If you love your husband enough to take care of his children, the love should be honored in both ways. If I marry her, I should be willing to love her children and treat all the children equally.

Karen: I think it's very difficult for the natural parent to watch the stepparent discipline the child. Maybe through the process of divorce or death, he or she has a sympathy for that child, of what that darling has gone through, and feels soft toward them. And as parents, we should feel soft towards our children. In this situation one parent has known the child longer; then the stepparent comes in, and his or her experience with that child has not been as great.

Dee: My husband and I have been in that situation.

I agree with what Karen said, and this is basically what we went through. I thought of what my children and I have been through and then thought, My husband couldn't understand.

Pastor Neyland: You will normally find that the problem is a lack of understanding. Where do you go when you need an answer? The husband and wife must come together. In a stepparent situation there can be no respecter of persons. Once a child sees that, it will lead to bitterness.

Cindy: I was in the same situation when Stan and I married. Before I married him I sat down and thought about what I wanted in my home life and how I wanted it to be. I didn't know a thing about children when I married Stan, so they had to learn with me and I had to learn with them. I thought about when Stan and I had a child together—what would I want for that child?—and I decided I wanted to make sure that April and Jonathan had everything that I would want for a child I would have with Stan.

What I appreciated in Stan was that he wanted me to love his children, but love is also discipline. He didn't tell me, "Love my children but don't discipline them." He asked me to love them one-hundred percent, and he allowed me that room. I know without a doubt I've made mistakes with the children. I've gone to them several times and said, "I'm sorry, I was too hard" or "I'm sorry, I shouldn't have done that." Stan didn't jump on me and say "Oh, you don't love them, you mean stepmother. You hate my children." He never did that with me. I think the natural parent has to understand that the new parent doesn't know much about what they are doing and decide to make allowances for that. If the stepparent is willing to pray and is doing the very best that he or she can, then the stepparent is not going to hurt the child. The stepparent will try so hard that he or she will actually go overboard to be a perfect parent.

Karen: We were talking earlier about house rules, and I think there also need to be firm rules for when children don't obey. What happens then? It is easy to react in anger. Continuity is important. Both parents need to go by rules.

Karl: Discipline should be consistent. If something is wrong one day, it should be wrong every day.

Pastor Neyland: Inconsistency frustrates the child. Is God inconsistent with us? There is a difference between breaking a spirit (or will) and crushing it. Hebrews 12:6 tells us, "Whom the Lord loveth he chasteneth." God chastens to break our self-will, for it is in our spirit to rebel.

Question: The purpose of discipline of children is to . . .

Karen: Instill respect for authority.

Ed: Establish boundaries and a secure lifestyle, so they know where they stand.

Myrna: Show that there are negative consequences for bad behavior.

Chris: Train the child.

Jesus Had a Stepfather
God has a lot of confidence in stepparents, for Jesus had a stepfather. Joseph, the stepfather of Jesus, played

an important role in history. God handpicked Joseph to love, protect, and instruct His only Son. Not just any man could have been a stepfather to Jesus.

Not just any woman can step into a broken family and with God's help put the pieces back together again. If you are a woman whom God is using for this purpose, I challenge you to see your role through God's eyes. You are important to your family! If you are the wife in a home with children, then you are a mother. Fill the position with prayer.

God sees your family and their needs. He sees their desires and hopes. You are the woman who can meet their needs, encourage them to dream, and help them reach their potential.

Yes, your situation is unique. Yes, there are struggles. Yes, you must make adjustments that other families could never understand. I understand your difficulties and your frustrations. But, like Joseph, you are chosen by God. Mother, fall in love with your family. You have a job to do, and God has confidence in you. Problems are temporary, but children are eternal souls.

❤️❤️❤️❤️❤️ *6* ❤️❤️❤️❤️❤️❤️

Understanding Your Children

Many times we assume we know why children behave the way they do and what they are thinking. In fact, we assume many things without really knowing for sure. Often the reason we don't know how the child feels is because we fail to ask. We are so busy analyzing the child that we forget to ask.

Under the privacy of changed names and with the promise never to tell Mom or Dad what they said, let me share the feelings, opinions, and thoughts of children just like yours. Some are young, some are teenagers. Many were from Christian homes; a few were from homes where divorce left them with one Christian parent and one unsaved parent. Some had good relationships with their stepparent; most did not. Perhaps you will hear what your child is speaking through one of these children.

Question: How did you feel when you found out that

your dad was going to get married?

Nicole: I was glad! I was happy that I would have a mother again.

Christie: My dad hasn't married yet, but I hate it already.

Jennifer: I was happy.

Question: What are the advantages in your dad's remarrying?

Lisa: My dad was lonely, but since he married he is a lot happier.

James: One good thing about my dad getting married is maybe I can have a brother now.

Deanna: I didn't have to go to a babysitter anymore when my dad went to work.

Nicole: I had a mom to take me shopping for clothes.

Question: How do you feel about your stepmom?

Jennifer: I want to be her friend, but I think she is jealous of me. She loves her child more than she loves me and it shows.

Nicole: One time in the car before the wedding we asked if we could call her Mom and she said we could. After that I have always thought of her as Mom.

Christie: My future stepmom really ticks me off because she makes me feel left out. She wants everything to be just her and my dad.

Question: What advice would you give children in your situation so they could get along with their stepmom?

Jennifer: Be helpful. Talk to your stepmom; don't be closed up. If she doesn't start conversations, then you start it.

Nicole: Just love your new mom and try to help her

out. She is coming into a situation that is difficult.

Question: What advice would you give to the new mother coming into a family?

Christie: Don't act like it is a pain to have the children around.

Nicole: Try to include the children like you would if they were your own children, because they will feel left out and feel like you don't love them. This may sound silly, but take care of them, because God gave them to you to take care of.

Question: Do you have any last thoughts you want to share?

Deanna: People take the joy out of having a brother or sister because they always think you're jealous. If people didn't point out to you that you are jealous or you should be jealous then I wouldn't even think about it.

Nicole: That's true. By saying, "Aren't you jealous?" then you start thinking, Yeah, I'm going to be jealous.

Jennifer: I can dress myself and feed myself. Anyone with common sense knows that my baby sister needs more attention. A person who watches other people and looks for jealousy has probably never lived in a house with a baby.

James: My last thought is to the new stepmom. Don't be Mr. Nice Guy when the Dad is around and then be mean when Dad goes to work.

Christie: I'm afraid if my dad has other kids I'll just be an outsider.

Nicole: I'm really glad my dad got married. I don't remember many things about my first mother, and I feel like Mom was my real mom from the start. I feel that she really loves me.

Let's look further into some of the complaints or fears of these children.

- "She loves her child more than she loves me."
- "She wants everything to be just her and my dad."
- "Don't act like it is a pain to have the children around."
- "Don't be Mr. Nice Guy when Dad is around and then be mean when Dad goes to work."
- "I'm afraid if my dad has other kids I'll just be an outsider."

When Christie expressed her fear of being an outsider she summed up the feeling in most of the other statements. We all fear rejection. We all fear loss of security. As adults we may think that these children are being irrational to fear rejection, but when dealing with a child to whom the worst (death or divorce) has already happened, we can't simply say, "Don't be silly. You aren't an outsider." Only love, attention, and building a solid foundation of family unity will dismiss what we may term childish fears.

If you have children with your husband, think of how you would want a stepmother to treat your birth child. Is the way you are treating your stepchild what you would want for your birth child? Is your attitude toward this child Christ-like? Can you be a Christian and not have the right attitude toward your stepchild?

It is reasonable to want time alone with your new husband. It is also reasonable to make a child feel good about the time that you and your husband are spending together, not make the child feel like an unwanted visitor.

If you want time alone with your husband, plan a special time for your child. Use a babysitter that your child enjoys spending time with, or allow your child to invite a friend over for the evening. Plan games and prepare snacks. Make the evening for the child seem twice as exciting as the evening you and Dad will be having.

Don't be secretive with the child. If your child has lost one parent, he may be afraid of losing a second parent. April used to beg Stan to stay home from work. She was afraid he would die, too. She only felt secure when her daddy was home. Tell your child where you are going, how long you plan to be gone, and that you have left your phone number with the sitter in case something important happens. If you are going to be later than planned, telephone home and reassure your child.

Consistency in your behavior with your child is a must. As James said, "Don't be Mr. Nice Guy until Dad goes to work." Don't be a phony. You can only keep up an act for so long, and then the strain of everyday living will bring reality to the surface. If you are mean when Daddy leaves, rest assured that Daddy and anyone else who will listen will soon hear about it from the children.

Be pleasant. Your mood will set the mood of the home.

When it is time to add to the family, do so without diminishing the importance of the other children. Jonathan, having been the baby for so long, had a harder time adjusting to the idea of a new baby in the family. April was delighted. She had prayed long and hard for this. Before we decorated a nursery we did a little redecorating on Jonathan's room. We put a wallpaper border around the wall and bought a matching lamp. It was not difficult and not too costly. Certainly it was worth it if it made Jonathan feel better about the baby. I referred to the baby as our baby, and I took the children to the doctor with me to listen to the heartbeat and see the baby via ultrasound. We looked through name books together, and I asked for their opinion on everything from decorating to birth announcements to who should be the first to know when baby arrived. I asked for their opinion, but I let them know in advance that Daddy and I had the final say, so they wouldn't feel slighted if we didn't take their advice. The point is, include your children in preparing for the new baby.

Many of the fears children have can be alleviated by compassion, common sense, and a Christian attitude. Many of the children I talked with started out with a positive feeling about Dad's remarrying and ended up with hurts or disappointments. You can't redo the past, but you can erase it by making the present and future a happy, loving life.

Stepfamilies result from loss. There must be a time for the child to grieve for the lost parent or for the lost family unit. It has been estimated that creating a healthy family relationship can take three to seven years.

Together, do not push yourself or the title of Mother on the children. Give the child time and reasons (by your actions) to accept and love you. Pray for a bonding between you and the child. Be available for the child, but also realize that some children will never look to you as Mom. In that case, be content with a wonderful friendship.

Instill a proper self-esteem in your child. Failure to

do so can help lead to tragedy. As an example, here is what Patricia Bissell wrote about the death of her son due to a drug overdose. (Taken from "They Dared Cocaine and Lost," *Reader's Digest,* May 1988, p. 87.)

> We are quick to blame such tragedies on others— on peer pressure, stressful occupations, drug dealers, everyone except ourselves. But most of these problems begin at home, when children are being brought up. It is hard for me to admit this, but I failed to nurture in Patrick the self-esteem he needed to deal with life. No matter how well he did, he felt that he had failed. He used drugs because they allowed him to escape that feeling. When we come to understand and accept this aspect of addiction, maybe we can do something about it.

A child does not have the "right" to make a decision that is destructive to his spiritual, mental, physical, or emotional well-being or the well-being of those around him. God has given decision-making rights to the parents. Use them wisely. Do not hesitate to say no in order to remove your child from spiritual dangers.

If you are willing to correct or discipline a child, then you should be just as quick to praise and hug that child. If you do, the child will not resent you for disciplining him when he has done wrong. He will feel secure in the boundaries of your love. The rest of the world is very critical, so give your children praise, make them feel good about themselves, and build their confidence.

If you are a wise parent you will realize that your child is an individual. He was given certain abilities, attributes, and gifts; he has his own unique personality; he came with likes and dislikes; and his physical appearance is all his own.

Only by studying and observing will you get to know this child. Ask God for wisdom and understanding in every matter concerning your child. Spend time watching, talking with, and listening to your child. As you do so, you will be able to make intelligent decisions concerning the future of your child.

♥♥♥♥♥♥♥ *7* ♥♥♥♥♥♥♥

The Two-Family Child

Dear Cindy,
I know that the women who write to you whose husband's first wife is no longer living will probably strike you in a very personal way. I'm sure they will have a lot of good (and bad) experiences to share.

I just wanted to ask that you consider the problems of the women for whom the first wife is still alive. Please do not take our case lightly.

Love, Donna

Dear Donna,
You are right, we do tend to minister in areas that are most near to our hearts or areas that we have experienced. Thanks for pointing this out. Because of your beautiful example of a successful "full-time mother to a part-time child" I have taken what I have seen you practice and all your thoughts you so freely shared with me on this subject and used them in this chapter.

Love, Cindy

*I*n interviewing women on the problems and solutions to sharing custody of children, I found that there were more problems than solutions. One solution could not possibly apply to every situation. In cases of serious problems, I strongly urge you to seek the counsel of your pastor. I cannot give you the answer to your particular problem, but perhaps I can help you as you seek out the best for your family.

The Previous Spouse

Problem: His ex-wife ruins our plans with her constant change of schedules.

Problem: We are constantly under pressure for more child support. His one child gets more money spent on him than our two little ones together.

Problem: Our visitations with the child are steadily being reduced almost to the point of being nonexistent.

Problem: My husband's ex-wife always wants to call my husband at work or meet with him alone to discuss problems or needs of their children. I feel that I should be included.

Answer: I cannot address all the serious problems that can arise when the present wife begins to feel used or abused by the ex-wife. However, there are ways to relieve the tenseness of the situation.

First and foremost, pray! In order to handle your problem in a Christian manner you need God's help and wisdom.

Second, communicate with your spouse. It is best to have your game plan worked out ahead of time, but if a crisis arises, stay calm. Express your opinions on the situation, but this is no time to argue with your spouse. Focus on the problem at hand, not on all the problems you have had to deal with since you first got married. Do not blame or punish your husband for the behavior of his ex-wife!

Most importantly, keep in mind the welfare of the child. This child's spiritual, physical, and emotional well-being is a top priority. You cannot take out your frustrations on that child or allow him to feel that he is the cause of all your problems. You chose to marry this man knowing that he had a responsibility to his children. These children are now your responsibility, too.

There are not easy solutions to every problem. Some problems will always be there as long as the ex-wife is alive. While I cannot solve your problems, let me share a few ideas on what will not work.

- *Anger.* It will only blow the problem out of proportion. Anger is an exaggerator.
- *Arguing* with your husband. You must be a team. Show a united front.
- *Resenting* your husband for having an ex-wife and children.
- *Bitterness* has never solved a problem yet.
- *Playing* the role of a martyr.

The Children

Problem: My stepdaughter resents me. She was the apple of Daddy's eye until I came along. She hates sharing her dad.

Problem: My stepchildren have no respect for me

because my husband does not require it.

Problem: My husband refuses to enforce our household rules because he is afraid the children will not want to come and visit him.

Problem: When I discipline the children they answer me with, "You aren't my mother so I don't have to mind you."

Problem: I dreamed of being a family, but my stepson tells me I am an intruder.

Problem: I'm in a no-win situation. If I discipline the children, my husband and other family members think of me as the wicked stepmother. If I do something extra special for the children, then I'm accused of trying to play up to the kids.

Answer: Weekend parenting is much tougher than full-time parenting. Yes, the hours are shorter, but the time is emotionally charged. Everyone is looking out for self or trying to keep peace.

Again, it is your attitude that will determine the outcome of a bad situation. You cannot force your children to love you, but you can love them unconditionally as Christ has loved you. Let me share what men and women who have overcome these problems say.

Donna: I sat down one day and thought about this child and how I felt about him (love, hate, frustration). I thought about how I should feel about him. Could I handle the challenges and problems he had brought into my life? How much responsibility was I willing to take on for him above and beyond the call of duty? I came to the conclusion that God had given me to him and him to me for a reason. I prayed as I pondered, and I began to feel a very strong spiritual responsibility for this child.

Most fathers are quite busy and don't always take the time to be sensitive to the needs of their children, and my husband, the father of this child, was not an exception. The mother had walked away from God when she had walked away from her marriage, taking this little one with her. If the mother didn't care and the father didn't have much time, who was going to teach and train this child to grow up to love and serve God? It didn't take long to figure that one out!

I began to do my best to fulfill my spiritual responsibility, and as I reached out to this child with more of my time and love (the more his mother dated the more time I had to spend with him), anger and resentment over this "obligation" began to melt away. I also began to see needs in other areas of his life that I could meet: emotional (I'm sorry you feel lonely tonight. How about snuggling up with me on the sofa and we will read some books together?) and physically (I'm cooking this big dinner because earlier he showed me the prizes he got from eating dinner at McDonalds three times this week).

I am not saying that things were perfect after that, but when I began to see things in a better perspective, these problems were easier to deal with. Instead of feeling used, I tried to see this time as another way to reach this child's soul.

Mary Lu: My stepdaughters' mother is not a Christian. I want to show them the difference in Christian living and sinful living. By my example as a Christian woman and mother, I believe that I can win them to Christ. I want them to see the advantages in being a Christian. I don't belittle their mother, and I don't compete with her. I accept their mother's place in their lives, but by being a friend and truly loving the girls, I have a place in their lives and hearts.

Mark: When Karen and I returned from our honeymoon the full responsibility of parenting was waiting for me. I went into our living room and I wept before the Lord, confessing to the Lord that I didn't know how to be a father. Like Solomon, I asked for wisdom. I determined that my main priority would be to serve the Lord. I wanted the children to have that example to follow.

There is a meshing process that these families go through, and it can't be rushed. There is quite a bit of adjusting in every area. Love means a lot more than words; it involves action.

We can't run away from or wish away these problems. Raising a family is hard, but the closer we stay to God, the easier it is.

Let us summarize the advice that experienced parents in two-family situations have shared. (1) Put God first. (2) Ask God for wisdom. (3) Love your child to the saving of his or her soul.

Sometimes we put stress in our lives that does not have to be there. Getting tense and dreading the weekend visit of your child is certainly not conducive to a good time for anyone. It is better to relax.

You are with your spouse much more than the child is. Be mature enough to share cheerfully. Children need both parents. Encourage your husband to plan times alone with the children.

When you truly love a child, it hurts when, in a moment of anger or disappointment, he says, "You aren't my mom." But remember that you are the adult. Don't come down to the child's level and try to hurt him by responding, "No, thank the Lord, I'm certainly not." You can try answering, "No, I am not your mother, but I love you and I am responsible for you. I am doing this because I want what is best for you."

You can only be as much of a parent as your spouse will allow you to be and as you are willing to be.

Be compassionate. Put yourself in the place of your husband and in the place of your new children.

House rules are important, but not if the rules destroy the purpose of the home. Someone once asked me, "What good are manners at mealtime if the sharing of family time is destroyed by correcting and nagging?" I agree that furniture must not be destroyed, but what rules are you willing to bend in order to ensure a peaceful visit? If the house is a little messy, are you willing to overlook it in order to allow for a happy, productive family weekend?

Before you complain, examine yourself. Are your complaints valid, or are they motivated by jealousy, feelings of neglect, or resentment? Be woman enough to rise above childish behavior such as pouting, sulking, or telling on the children.

Home Away from Home

Here he comes with his little suitcase. It is his

weekend with Daddy. Setting his suitcase down in the hall, he looks in the family room to see Daddy's other children playing with their toys. Since it is late, it will soon be bedtime. While Les and Lori go to their rooms and get ready for bed, Joey must change into his pajamas in the bathroom. Then he will wait for his cot to be put up. Joey sleeps in the family room.

My sister did not want the foregoing scenario for her stepson. Chris had his own room. His closet was full of his clothes. The toy box held his very own toys. On his bed were his favorite stuffed animals. When Chris came for a visit he was coming home. It was his second home, but Donna made sure he could call it home.

I encourage you to make your home truly a home to the children. If space is a problem, at least find a closet they can call their very own, a place where they can leave play clothes and church clothes, toys and books, a favorite game or stuffed animal.

Being a Full-Time Parent
to a Part-Time Child

Be as involved in the life of your child as possible. If the ex-wife is uncooperative, meet with your child's teacher at school and express a desire to be informed of your child's progress or problems. Leave stamped, self-addressed envelopes with the teacher in order to encourage her to correspond. Ask the school office to mail you a copy of the child's report cards and a calendar of the school events. If you live close enough, try to attend open-house meetings.

If you live quite a distance from your child, write and

send pictures of family and events regularly. Call as often as finances allow. If you can't attend the special events in your child's life such as a role in the school play, telephone beforehand and express your confidence in him, and if possible telephone again after the event to hear all the details.

Keep all your promises. Breaking promises to a child will cause the child to view you as a liar. The child will lose confidence in you. Of course, emergency situations will arise and children understand this, but consistently broken promises cause little hearts to be consistently broken. Don't make a promise unless you are sure you can keep it.

Make your part-time child as much a part of your home as your other children. Display pictures of the child. Take family pictures. Put artwork on the refrigerator. Write on the calendar special events or activities that the child is participating in.

Listen when your child wants to talk. Many adults do not have the patience to listen to childish ramblings or adolescent day dreams, but shared confidences and true interest in what your child is saying mean more than all the big trips to Disneyland. If you are available to listen to the childish ramblings or adolescent daydreams, then your child knows you will be there to encourage him when he is discouraged, to instruct or counsel him during difficult times with peers, to pray with him in times of spiritual battle, and to rejoice with him when he succeeds.

An advertisement once read, "The bedtime story is more important than the bed." If your child will allow you, depending on his or her age, make bedtime a special time.

Read a bedtime story and talk or make plans for the next day. Before you turn off the lights and leave the room, remember to pray together, hug the child, and say, "I love you."

No matter how old the child is, before everyone goes to bed you can pray together. When they were small I used to pray with April and Jonathan separately while holding them in my arms, and I thanked the Lord for giving them to me. I wanted them to realize that I thought of them as a gift from God. This makes your child feel special and loved.

Accepting the Unacceptable

You may say, "All of your ideas sound sweet and cozy, but my stepchildren hate me. Those ideas would never work in our home." Sometimes, no matter how much you have prayed or how much effort you have put into loving someone, the problems in a stepchild's life overpower the relationship. If this is the case, in order to save yourself heartache and stress, you should accept the children and the situation for what they are and leave it to God to do the changing. Sometimes we try too hard, while sometimes we really haven't tried at all. Only you and God really will know how much you have put into making a successful relationship with your stepchild. If you have done all you could do and there is only a bad relationship, it is better to prayerfully resign yourself to the situation. On the weekends that your stepchild visits, try to involve yourself in a hobby or go to the shopping mall with a friend, leaving time for your husband and his child to be together. Do this cheerfully. Never stop praying for peace and acceptance. God is still a miracle worker.

In conclusion you won't be able to change your husband, your stepchildren, or the ex-wife, but you can change your attitude. Take the following steps

1. *Pray for wisdom and understanding.*

2. *Be kind and compassionate.* Put yourself in the place of your spouse and his child.

3. *Concentrate on the good.* Look for the positive. Most people are about as happy as they make up their minds to be. Make up your mind to make each day a happy day for your spouse, your children, and yourself.

8

Creating a Family and Building a Home

*T*he dictionary defines the word *family* as "1. A social group consisting of a husband, a wife, and a child or children; 2. A household; relatives living in one home." One definition of the word *home* is "the family unit."

"Stepfamilies" are real families. We are social groups that consist of a husband, wife, and child or children. We are challenged to build a home for this family. The following passages of Scripture express some principles for doing so.

- *Except the LORD build the house, they labour in vain that build it: except the LORD keep the city, the watchmen waketh but in vain* (Psalm 127:1).
- *Through wisdom is an house builded; and by understanding it is established* (Proverbs 24:3).

• *And if a house be divided against itself, that house cannot stand* (Mark 3:25).

• *And the rain descended, and the floods came, and the winds blew, and beat upon that house; and it fell not: for it was founded upon a rock* (Matthew 7:25).

• *Every wise woman buildeth her house: but the foolish plucketh it down with her hands* (Proverbs 14:1).

Ultimately, people build houses; God builds homes.

Family Traditions

Creating a family means creating a special, one-of-a-kind, this-is-the-way-we-do-things-in-our-home lifestyle. Celebrating holidays or birthdays, making up special occasions, and just everyday ways of doing things make memories for you and your children. Bonding a family can be done by doing special things together and recording them.

Some family traditions are simple; some are a little more involved. Here are a few ideas from various people. Start with these and then use your own imagination.

• At Christmas I always sign our Christmas cards using all five of the children's names. The three oldest live with their mother, but I want people to think of us as a unit, not two separate families. As an added benefit, by doing so people include all our children when they address the cards they send us. When the children arrive for their holiday visit they notice and feel more a part of us because of it. This is a good practice for any card or gift given on special occasions from the family.

• When our third child (my first baby) was born, I wanted pictures of him everywhere. In order not to make my older children feel less important, I made sure their pictures were also placed in strategic locations.

• Have complete family portraits made as often as possible. Give each child a framed picture to put in his or her room.

• When I first married, my husband's teenaged niece lived with us. On the mornings that I served the children breakfast in bed I made a tray for her also. Later, after she had moved, she told me that by doing things for her that I did for the children she felt my love and acceptance of her as part of my family.

• I have boxes of Christmas ornaments. One box contains our family ornaments and the other three are for the children. They each have their own box, and every Christmas I add two or three ornaments to their collection. I put their name and year on each one in order to keep track of which one belongs to each child. When they are grown they will have a set of memories and a tradition to carry with them.

• Have a special meal that you serve for a holiday. My family always had Mexican food for Christmas dinner. I want to carry that on with my children.

• We sometimes have a party for no special reason, or we look for a reason. Our favorite is a welcome home party when Dad comes in from work. We decorate his chair with balloons and streamers, make funny pictures and cards, and serve popcorn with soda or something equally easy to get together at the last minute. Usually our parties are done on the spur of the moment.

• Rick's daughter is fifteen, but we always wait until she joins us for Easter to create baskets. Each of us participates in dyeing eggs, and when they are dry we divide the eggs and candy and take a basket to create. After we are done, I set the baskets on the table and put books, crayons, pen, and pencils—gifts according to the children's ages—in them. On Easter morning we each have a basket waiting for us at our place at the breakfast table.

Starting Traditions

When you marry into a family you will find certain traditions that are an established part of the family. You will also bring traditions with you that were part of your past. The challenge is to blend these traditions. These blended traditions are what will become precious memories to your children and what they will carry into marriage with them.

I love family traditions. I enjoy making holidays special and events unforgetable. When and how to celebrate is up to you, but by all means find several times each year to make memories and carry on a tradition. For example, mark the following special dates in red on an annual calendar.

New Year's Day	Father's Day
Valentine's Day	July Fourth
Easter	Back to School
Mother's Day	Labor Day
Memorial Day	Thanksgiving
End of School	Birthdays

How do you celebrate? We have Mexican food on Christmas Eve. I like a special breakfast on Valentine's

Day and Easter. The Fourth of July is a time for a backyard barbeque with the family. We celebrate the return of school days with a children's party. On and on the list goes. We have tradition with a twist of something new or different to add spice and excitement to the occasion.

Interview your family to find out what they like best about the holidays. What do they want to do every year? What are their greatest memories? Take those and plan the holidays around them this year.

Enjoy family times. Think of ways to make your family unique. Celebrating together is fun, and it creates a family bond.

Record each celebration in a diary and with pictures. Reminiscence together.

Traditions should be fun for the family. It isn't necessary to carry on a tradition that everyone hates. If your mom served brown beans and cornbread for Christmas dinner and your family hates brown beans, go ahead and serve the Chinese food they love instead.

Don't be frustrated if an idea doesn't seem to catch on. Traditions are years in the making, and time only perfects them.

Serving Your Family

Our family should be our top priority. It is a pity that many times we save the best in our home for company. The most important people in our lives are often treated as if they were less important than the visitor or stranger.

Am I the only one who saves the fine china for holidays and adults? We are all guilty of trying to impress our guests and not feeling the importance of impressing our family. The message we sometimes send to our children is "You aren't as important as the stranger."

To be thoughtful is to anticipate the needs and wants of others, to be full of concern. Our families should be the first to receive VIP treatment. Here are a few ideas for serving your family.

• Send your family off to work or school with "I love you and I'm praying for you" ringing in their ears.

• Pack their lunches with more than food. On a piece of paper write a love note or a favorite verse of Scripture, or if time doesn't permit, then draw a happy face.

• Cut out a cartoon and tape it where the recipient is sure to find it.

• Everyone loves to receive mail. Send a card or letter to each member of your family. Homemade cards add a very special love touch.

• Dinner prepared and served with thoughtfulness shows love. Use place mats. Get out the fine china and crystal. Light candles. What's the special occasion? You are all home together!

• Reward your family with breakfast in bed some morning, or while your children are studying or your husband is reading, prepare a little snack tray and carry it to them.

• Make every holiday an event to remember.

• Send thank-you notes to your family for the nice things they do for you.

• Reward good behavior with praise and appreciation.

We must make time to show concern and appreciation, and pay attention to tasks well done. People try harder when they know someone cares. People love to be loved!

Creating an Atmosphere

Have you ever walked into a home where it felt good to come through the door? Maybe there was an aroma of cinnamon rolls baking in the oven. You could hear gospel music playing on the stereo in the family room. The mother of the home was singing along while she worked in the kitchen. The house was clean and friendly. There was a peaceful feeling in every room.

Then there are homes that seem to be in a constant state of confusion. Children are arguing and Mother is screaming at them to stop. She seems as out of control as the children. The house is not really dirty but it isn't clean either. Clutter is everywhere. The phone rings, dinner is boiling over on the stove, and tempers are boiling over with it. You wish you had never come.

Obviously we all want our home to be like the first one I described, but that takes effort. You, mother, will create the atmosphere of the home. If you are lazy, the children will be lazy. If you scream, the children will scream louder. If you are out of control, every part of your life will reflect that.

My mother taught me that, when situations seemed overpowering and I was losing my cool, I should find a private place and take authority over the situation and my spirit, rebuking confusion and anger in Jesus' name.

Ask the Lord to bring peace into the home and into your mind. It works. If you want a cheerful family then you must set the pace by being cheerful yourself.

Keep a spirit of praise. Your mind and spirit will be refreshed if you have praise music playing in your home. Talk to the Lord as you work. Jesus is a good listener! Don't be embarrassed to praise the Lord as you do the chores around your home. What a beautiful example it is to your children!

One day the children were extremely irritable from being kept inside due to heavy snow. I was even more cranky than the children. The children were bored. I felt lonely because Stan was at work and I couldn't get out of the house. The more the day wore on, the more our nerves were on edge. Realizing the situation was getting out of control, I decided to do something drastic. I called April and Jonathan downstairs. I told April to bring her tambourine, and I gave Jonathan a pan and a wooden spoon to use for a drum. Then the three of us marched through the house in follow-the-leader style singing every church song we could think of. It was silly but it worked.

Take authority over the atmosphere in your home. You are in control. Don't allow bad moods or rotten attitudes to spoil the atmosphere.

After a day of struggle in the workplace or school, home should be the first place your family wants to run to, not from.

Family Devotions

It is true that children learn by example. I learned to pray as a small child because my mother didn't allow me to run and play during prayer time. When it was time to pray I was sitting by my mom while she prayed for several hours.

Today I appreciate that my mom taught me by her example. Your children will also look back on their childhood with appreciation if you have taken the time to teach them about God and given them an example to follow in Christian living. My husband remembers as a small boy the secure feeling he would have during family prayer times as he knelt by his mother and listened to her pray.

Family devotions are often neglected in modern homes. Too often we depend on the church or the pastor to do our work for us. We can find many excuses as to why we don't take the time to pray and study the Bible with our children, but when it is all said and done our excuses are pretty feeble. I encourage you to set a time and place for regular devotions in your home. Take the phone off the hook and don't allow anything to interrupt this precious time.

The father is the spiritual leader, but if he can't lead devotions due to work, or if he simply won't, then, mother, take upon yourself the responsibility of seeing your children grow in God's Word.

Family devotions need not be long to be effective. Keep interest high. Read the Bible with your children, but pause after a verse or passage and discuss what it means. Make sure the child understands, or he will be bored. Make family devotions fun. Think of a game to play or songs to sing that will help the children remember what they learned from the Bible that night. Act out a story from the Bible. Have your children memorize a passage of Scripture and do artwork to illustrate that passage. Play records or tapes and sing along. If you are musically inclined, gather the family around the piano to sing and worship.

A successful devotion is one that meets the needs of your family. It is a success if you and your children have been encouraged and uplifted. It is a success if your children have grown in truth.

Talk to other families or go to your Christian bookstore for more ideas on exciting family devotions.

Remember, you will have to guard this time. The devil will consistently work against this powerful home-building tool.

♥.♥.♥.♥.♥.♥.♥.♥. 9 ♥.♥.♥.♥.

In-Laws and Out-Laws

*T*his chapter discusses relationships with your spouse's previous in-laws ("out-laws") and your new in-laws. Here are some issues we will consider.

Previous In-Laws

• Your attitude towards them and their relationship with your spouse

• Loving them and accepting them

• Drawing lines of privacy and setting guidelines for reliving the past

• Still a part of your family

New In-Laws

• Their acceptance of you

• Friendship with the previous spouse'

Let me present a few of the problems that many have faced in their new marriage. After we present the problems we will talk about solutions.

Jan: It took almost a year before my husband drew lines for his former in-laws and said, "Don't step over this boundary." Before it was a free-for-all in reminiscing, storytelling, and comparing. It started the first Sunday we returned from our honeymoon. My husband's former father-in-law was the adult Bible class teacher, and during the class he brought up his daughter and many of her wonderful abilities and qualities. He would interject each praise with, "You can ask Joe" (my husband) or "Wasn't she, Joe?" I didn't say anything for fear that people would think I was overreacting, but I should have realized then what was ahead.

(Note: Jan didn't say a word about the "praise service" the previous in-law was having for his daughter and asking Jan's husband to join. I have found that if you say, "That makes me uncomfortable or I feel like I'm being unfavorably compared," people often label you as jealous, oversensitive, or insecure. On the other hand, if you don't speak up for yourself, then people will proceed to do as they please while you hurt on the inside but bravely smile on the outside. You must decide if you would rather wear a label or keep your hurt hidden.)

Nancy: I have encountered some resentment from the former in-laws on my first few visits with them. It was about small things that didn't amount to much but nevertheless made me very uncomfortable. Since my husband was very close to this family, I was concerned about it and pointed it out to him. Alan insisted that the family would be a family to me and love me as one of them. He could not see the problems because he didn't want there to be any. His love for them made him loyal to what seemed to me to be a lost cause. I felt hurt many times when they would do things or make comments that, out of his loyalty to them, he would defend or justify. I felt that he thought I was making these problems up purposely to cause a rift. Only after several years and one sister-in-law confessed to the deeds did he really see the situation as it actually was.

Clare: The hardest part of my adjustment to having a previous family in my life was the way I was always introduced to new people who would visit our church. My husband and I attended the same church as some previous in-laws, and whenever we had visitors I was introduced with, "This is Clare, Bob's new wife." Bob's first wife had died in a car accident five years before. There I would stand, waiting for this endless and very unnecessary explanation to finish. I longed to be accepted as Clare, Bob's wife. The long, detailed explanation made me feel as though they wanted everyone to know that the only reason I was here was because of their tragedy. I wanted to be a person who was accepted and didn't have to be explained.

Marcia: My hardest times were those when Mark was not around. This gave my new family ample opportunity to share with me the great love stories of Mark and his first wife. They would fill me in on her many abilities (which they had noticed I didn't seem to have) and correct me on all my parenting efforts. I cried for the first six months of my marriage. My self-confidence was almost gone, and I had no doubt that my husband did not love me. If he did, why would he allow me to be continually abused emotionally and verbally? Mark would come home and I would relate the latest incident, in tears of course, and his only reaction would be, "They didn't mean it." That was a small comfort to me. Besides, why would they keep saying something if they didn't mean it?

(Note: In order to keep things in perspective, we need to remember that our hurt is also our husband's hurt. If something affects us, it will certainly affect our spouse. At different times in my own adjustments, I felt that I was the only one who hurt. Stan corrected my thinking. Remember, your spouse is caught in the middle.)

Darlene: I don't believe that my husband's former in-laws disliked me as a person, but for three years after the death of their daughter and sister they could pretend that she was just away and not gone forever. When I came, I brought reality. All of a sudden there was this woman living in her house, raising her children, and loving and being loved by her husband. One sister-in-law said, "I can't help myself. I want my sister back in her house with her husband and children." Can you blame them?

Barbara: We did not have a lot of contact with my husband's former in-laws, but when we did, it was always a time of mixed emotions. On the one hand, they would try to include me and make me feel as though I were a part of the family, but on the other hand, they would make a negative remark about me, my marriage, or my parenting skills. Still, the good outweighed the bad.

(Note: This type of treatment is not always limited to former in-laws. Gina shared with me that her new mother-in-law had adored her former daughter-in-law. Everything Gina did could not compare to Ruth. When Ruth died, Gina's mother-in-law had helped Sam raise little Josh. Gina had to gain the respect of her new mother-in-law, not only in parenting but in every other area of her life. When Sam's mother came to visit, she criticized Gina's housekeeping and cooking. She took her to task for not being as stylish as Ruth. She expressed amazement that Sam could live with Gina after having a wife as good as Ruth. Sam felt for Gina but asked her to please respect his mother and in time she would accept her. He felt obligated to his mother because of all her help during the time he was a single parent with Josh.)

Interference with Discipline or Training

Anna: When my son would come home from each visit with his aunt, he would be confused about our house rules. When we would correct him for not doing the things we required and considered good manners, he would say, "But Aunt Emma said . . ." He was more afraid of displeasing Aunt Emma than displeasing me. My husband finally had to become very firm with Aunt Emma. Our new rule is, If other family members can't respect our guidelines for raising the children then their time alone with them will have to be cancelled until the children are older and won't be easily confused by the conflicting teaching. We must respect each other, but we are the parents, and what we say is what should matter to our children.

Lisa: My husband's father-in-law always said negative things to the children about me, such as, "You have a stupid mother. Look how she dressed you for church." Finally, I stopped feeling stupid, because when I looked around I wasn't any different from all the other mothers.

Karen: After the children and I had fully accepted our

new relationship, and I had become Mommy to them, we were at a celebration of a friend's engagement. At one point towards the end of the evening, someone who didn't know my children, me, or the situation, asked, "Whose little boy is that?" Without thinking I replied, "He is mine." My father-in-law immediately replied, "No, he is Jeff's." I was embarrassed, and in looking for a way to cover my awkwardness of the moment, I blurted out, "Well, who am I?" His reply crushed and humiliated me. He laughingly told me and the listening crowd, "You are nobody!" I was hurt because I knew he really felt that way about me. He had stripped me of my rights to my son and publicly humiliated me.

Custody Battles

Battles over the children from a previous marriage are not limited to parents. When someone has died, the family holds on with an even tighter grip. The children are all they have left of their daughter or sister.

Lydia: The grandparents, aunts, and uncles of Sarah come every Christmas for their annual visit. They come bearing gifts, and it is a great display of affection and tears. They cry because she looks like her "real" mother and feel they must give a detailed explanation of how she reminds them of her real mom. This is emotionally upsetting to the family. It causes division between Sarah's brother and sisters who have been added to our family. It drains me as the mother of them all, for while Sarah is flattered over the gifts and affection, being the center of attention leaves her confused. Her brother and sisters are jealous over the extravagant gifts and retaliate by excluding her from their circle. I hate the division they cause in my family.

Jenna: The former in-laws want the children for their holidays. What about "our" holidays? We want them to respect that as a family we have our own traditions we want to follow.

Grace Ann: What do you do when the aunts tell your children that you are trying to take them away from the family, when all you are doing is trying to be a normal family by spending time together?

How do you overcome . . .
. . . stories of the past
. . . people resenting you for unreasonable reasons
. . . negative feelings for your new family
. . . criticism

Let us look at some ways to respond to these situations. Time does heal wounds. Be willing to forgive and forget. Remember, everyone in the situation is hurting. Don't strike out in revenge. Overlook what you can. Show compassion.

One person told me that she could never live in the same town and attend the same church that her husband's former in-laws pastored. For some it would never work. For some it doesn't work because one or the other refuses to allow a friendship or respect to grow. Stop long enough to see what God can do. Maybe this is a time of character building in you. What good can God bring out of this situation?

When you think of your new extra set of in-laws, think

of their good points. Avoid situations that make you uncomfortable, but don't spend your life avoiding the family. If children are involved, like it or not, you will always be a part of their family.

Acceptance is the key. To accept people for what or who they are is a sign of a gracious woman. If your "outlaws" are willing to accept you with all of your faults, lessons to be learned, and victories to be won, then how much more should you be willing to do the same? In any case, don't try to change them. Learn to love them and allow them to love you. If someone extends a kind hand or makes gesture of friendship, please be quick to respond.

The Word of God brings us down to basics: "If a man say, I love God, and hateth [*Grosset Webster Dictionary:* 'to feel enmity or bitter aversion for; dislike intensely'] his brother, he is a liar: for he that loveth not his brother whom he hath seen, how can he love God whom he hath not seen? And this commandment have we from him, That he who loveth God love his brother also" (I John 4:20-21).

As Christians, Christ-like persons, it is our responsibility to show love toward others, even uncooperative "out-laws."

People often learn to love because of actions of others toward them. Based on your actions, how lovable are you?

Treat the "out-laws" with as much respect as you would your new in-laws. They are family.

I have always discussed each situation with Stan and respected whatever opinion he stated. I respected his opinion even though I didn't always agree with it. I have always stood in unity with all of his decisions.

Stand with your spouse. You are a team. Be unified.

Don't play tug of war with his loyalties. His first loyalty will be to you if he knows you are worthy of it. You may feel your partner has used poor judgment but support him as your partner and leader. Pray for him. Pray for your attitude in the situation. Commit the situation to God.

If the "out-laws" are against you and your spouse thinks that you are just being overly emotional or that you have a persecution complex, comfort yourself with the thought that the truth will eventually come out. By the same token, if you are being difficult and demanding behind your spouse's back, that will also come out. Jesus said, "For nothing is secret, that shall not be made manifest; neither any thing hid, that shall not be known and come abroad" (Luke 8:17).

In many cases our family members are Christians, but if they are not it is especially important to conduct ourselves uprightly so that by our actions they can be won to Christ. We also have a responsibility to be patient and kind toward fellow believers. "Forbearing one another, and forgiving one another . . . even as Christ forgave you, so do ye" (Colossians 3:13).

An old saying in Texas goes like this: "Hug your friends tight, but your enemies tighter; hug 'em so tight they can't wiggle." This is especially important in sticky family situations. Don't set out to make everyone your enemy but keep them close to you. Love them through difficult times. Working together is the only way to resolve differences.

There are always two sides to every story. While you may feel that you are reasonable to get along with, maybe your new family is having a hard time adjusting to the way you do things. My husband says that a match by itself does not create a flame. What causes the flame? Friction.

Constant advice or questioning from in-laws and "outlaws" can be frustrating. "Do you make the children brush their teeth?" "Don't let them eat that." "Do you know what soda will do to their bones?" In such cases, try to take the good; after all, none of us knows everything. Don't reject good advice because you resent the source. Show appreciation for advice, even if you never plan to use it. Why make hard feelings over something minor? Maybe the family isn't offering advice because they feel you are incompetent but because they need to feel involved in your children's lives.

Once again, I stress that there are two sides to every story. Learn to communicate your hurts. Attack the problem, not the people!

Let us therefore follow after the things which make for peace, and things wherewith one may edify another (Romans 14:19).

♥♥♥♥♥♥♥♥♥ 10 ♥♥♥

Handling Changes

Single life can be basically a self-oriented state of existence. The single adult usually spends his or her money on personal needs and wants.

To be thrust into marriage is a shock. You aren't spending your money on yourself anymore. Besides, your hubby doesn't see that new dress with an eighty-dollar price tag as a need! When you have a family you learn quickly that your motto is give, give, give!

How do you adjust without resentment? Some days you can't help but want to spend money to make yourself as attractive as possible. Just six months ago you would have headed for the nearest shopping mall with checkbook and credit cards tucked in your handbag. But today you are headed to the orthodontist with Susie, and tomorrow you will be at the mall doing business with the local shoe merchants but only because Janie is developing an ingrown toenail from improperly fitting shoes.

While self-sacrificing can be a tough adjustment, it has to come at some point in life. Now is time for responsibility.

Keep a good attitude during this time. All the designer outfits in the world won't make you attractive to your spouse if you are self-centered.

If you are a full-time homemaker, have self-respect and respect for your new ministry. Don't stay in a robe or gown all day. Get up and get dressed. If you plan on scrubbing floors all day wear something practical, but not something that makes you feel like a slob. Comb your hair. Wear a nice hairstyle; put in a bow or decorative comb. Don't put yourself down. Value your new job. Be creative in your approach to housework and cooking. Have fun!

Here are some tips for adjusting to your new role as homemaker.

• Try to do a little every day rather than allow jobs to grow. It is much easier to wash, dry, and put away one load of clothes per day instead of six loads of wash on Saturday.

• Don't let your leftovers go bad in the refrigerator. Have a meal of leftovers if necessary. At least your family won't be able to complain about a lack of variety when you serve a combination of several meals.

• Clean your kitchen immediately after a meal. It is hard to get motivated after you are sitting on the sofa enjoying a good book. Isn't it disheartening to walk into a kitchen that is a disaster? Especially if you allowed the food to cling to plates and pans all night. My mother-in-law washes as she cooks. By the time dinner is served there is very little left except the dishes on the table.

- If you have a dishwasher, start loading it the first thing in the morning with your breakfast dishes and keep adding until you have enough for a full load. It keeps your kitchen looking nicer.

- Be a creative cook. Experiment with recipes. I well remember my first meal as a new bride. I cooked dinner for my husband and two little food critics. It is intimidating when your first meal is greeted with looks of dislike or repulsion. Children are very vocal about your efforts. I asked myself a thousand times, "Why didn't you take a few cooking classes while you were in Paris?"

Now I have learned to give my children choices. I am teaching them the art of decision making. I say to them, "You don't have to eat it," and then the ball is in their court: Do I try this strange concoction sitting on the table, or do I starve the rest of the night?

I can't remember any big disasters. I must admit to praying over a casserole once before putting it in the oven. Whether the Lord "healed" it during baking or if it would have been a success anyway, I'll never know. The creator forgot how she created it and has not been able to duplicate it since. That, ladies, is creative cooking!

- Grocery shopping for a family is a lot different from shopping for one or two, or for a special meal for company. Let your husband be your guide. He will know better than you how much milk is consumed and how often you need to buy toilet paper. Plan menus and stay within a budget. If you make out a grocery list before you go shopping it will save unnecessary trips back to the store. It will also save on the purchase of duplicate items. And never go grocery shopping when you are hungry!

- If you use grocery coupons, put part or all of your savings in a special place. Use the money to buy something you want but are not financially able to purchase at the time. You worked for it. Believe me—using coupons is work! But it is well worth it when you come home with ten or twenty dollars in savings. That can add up fast!

- Make time in your day for prayer. In our busy lives, often the first thing we do is stop praying to allow time for eating, resting, work, and family. But Christ sacrificed eating, rest, and companionship to make time for prayer. The busier His schedule, the more He prayed.

- Take everything one day at a time. Blend gradually with your new family. Don't try to be a superwoman. Let your husband help you with the housework; he's been at it a long time.

- If your marriage has caused you to move to a new area, there is no need to be bored or lonely. Get to know your husband's friends. Invite couples in the church to your house. Initiate friendships at church and with neighbors, and get involved in local happenings. Take a class at a local community college, join an exercise class and attend, become a member of the local library. Get involved in your new church. Willing hands are always needed.

- A sense of humor is essential. Try to laugh at your mistakes (as well as learn from them). Don't agonize over yesterday; live happily today, and hope for a beautiful tomorrow.

- Don't let changes overwhelm you! Your first priority is your family; put your past lifestyle behind you. Friends must come second.

Most of us probably had an easy life of pleasing self

first and others second before marriage. If we were sick we stayed in bed, but now we must get out of bed and drag our body around the house while pretending to the family that we are functioning. Children get hungry even if we don't. Maybe you like to munch on a candy bar while reading a good book, and the constant "When are we going to eat dinner" still doesn't inspire you to cook. Yes, one is fun. Two is cozy. Three or more . . . that is a family!

In order to change your lifestyle you must change your way of thinking. You must think family not self. It is harder than it sounds, for years of putting self first becomes a habit. Then suddenly you have no place to hide when you are in a bad mood. If you try to find a quiet place to think or read or write letters you have a constant knocking on the door and little voices saying, "Mom, whatcha doing in there? When ya coming out, Mom?" I am a person who needs a certain amount of time alone to think. At first I found it very difficult to adjust to the fact that I could not retreat into my bedroom and stay there until I was good and ready to return to society. All of sudden there is someone else who has claim to your bedroom. Someone else has claim to your time.

Make time for yourself. You cannot sacrifice all your private times and pleasures. Go to the mall alone. Go for a drive. Occasionally have dinner at your favorite restaurant with a friend, or take only yourself and a good book. You deserve time to regroup.

It doesn't matter what crisis you will face or may already be in, God is with you. It is God's will for your marriage to last for life. A friend once told me that she hadn't prayed about God's choice in a husband and she now felt she had messed up her life and was completely out of God's will. But once a person marries it is God's will for him or her to make that marriage work. Divorce is not God's answer to a bad situation. God will be with you to help you make it work, and His joy will be your strength.

As with anything in life, the attitude you take will help determine the outcome of your situation. It will set the pace for your walk through a valley or the length of your stay on a mountaintop. We can choose an attitude of victory or defeat. We decide whether to say, "I can and I will" or "I give up—why bother?"

God knows where you are. Just because your address changed God hasn't lost track of you. "Whither shall I go from thy spirit? or whither shall I flee from thy presence? If I ascend up into heaven, thou are there: if I make my bed in hell, behold, thou art there. If I take the wings of the morning, and dwell in the uttermost parts of the sea; even there shall thy hand lead me, and thy right hand shall hold me" (Psalm 139:7-10). If you will trust in Him, He will enable you to handle the changes in your life and emerge victorious.

♥.♥.♥.♥.♥.♥.♥.♥.♥.♥.*11*.♥.♥.

The Spouse's Chapter

As I stood in the back of the banquet room watching the dispersing crowd say their final farewells I became aware that Ted, the special vocalist for the morning breakfast, was passing by. Stopping him I congratulated him on the beautiful songs he had chosen to sing. As we stood and talked, the question arose as to how each of us had come to attend a breakfast for the local chapter of Compassion Friends. Compassion Friends is a support group for parents who have lost their children. I explained that I had been invited along with my "number two mother-in-law" because she had lost her daughter, my husband's first wife, and had written a book on grief. I had shared her book with Marge, the lady who operated the dry cleaners by my house. Marge had lost her son in a car accident and through that event had become involved in Compassion Friends. Marge had invited us to come to their annual breakfast.

Ted seemed intrigued by my little explanation and questioned me extensively about my marriage, my relationship with my new children, and even my relationship with my husband's previous in-laws. My friendship with them seemed to astound him. Finally he explained the reason for his curiosity. Ted had been married to Ellen for nine years. They had lost two babies at birth, thus explaining his involvement with C.F., and then along came little Jessica. Unfortunately, during Ellen's pregnancy she was discovered to have a malignant cancer growth. Shortly after Jessica's birth Ellen passed away. Two years after Ellen's death Ted had remarried. Thus he requested, "Mrs. Miller, could you talk with my wife? The adjustments have been so hard for her. Maybe you could help her."

Introducing me to his petite bride with a brief explanation of my marriage, he said, "Talk to her, Pam. I'm sure she can help you." Ted patted Pam on the shoulder encouragingly and walked off.

Pam and I looked at each in an awkward silence for a brief moment, and then tears welled up in Pam's eyes. She poured out a story of a husband who was still grieving, a husband who compared their new marriage and her to a past marriage and a former wife. She shared the hurt of being rejected by a little girl who only wanted Daddy and a mommy she had never known. I realized it wasn't Pam who needed to talk, it was Ted who needed help. How I wish my husband had been there to minister to Ted!

My husband lost his wife of seven and one-half years to cancer. He was left to be both mother and father to a little girl who was five and a baby boy of twenty-two months. He was both breadwinner and homemaker. He juggled work, family, home, church, and his own grief and emotional crisis. Some days he was overwhelmed, but that is when he turned to God. God brought him through without bitterness, without anger, and with a beautiful attitude. He has a confidence in God that came through proving God in time of need. I felt if anyone was qualified to share thoughts on remarriage it was my husband. Here are his comments to those who have lost a spouse.

Walk carefully down this avenue in your life. Your life has been shattered via divorce or death, and it is the task of this new helpmate to help you put the scattered pieces to the puzzle of your life back together again. This is no easy job. She will need all the help, support, and understanding you can give her.

Being critical of the way she cooks, cleans, or takes care of the children will only complicate your marriage. I remember Cindy correcting the children and my thinking she was being too harsh. My first reaction was, I should jump to my children's defense. They really don't deserve this! Then I reasoned, She really loves the children; I know she does. I know that April and Jonathan feel loved by her. Still reasoning, I remembered the mistakes I had made years before as a new dad. I felt it was only fair to let their new mom learn the same way. Sometimes I think the children take their correction from the new mom better than the dad does!

How to correct the children and what is best for them can be a very volatile subject. It can lead to many arguments and lots of hard feelings. But love "thinketh no evil" and "vaunteth not itself." Let love do its perfect work in your marriage. As you work within the confines of love, your new bride will not use your children to vent her anger and frustrations. Every day it will become more "our" children and one family.

The apostle Paul said, "Forgetting those things which are behind . . . I press toward the mark" (Philippians 3:13-14). Even though I am applying this verse in a different context, I feel that it is wise for those entering into marriage for the second time to forget the past, in respect to comparing past experiences, especially if they are prone to compare marriages. The mark they should press toward —the prize they want—is a warm, happy home where love is not only defined and discussed but shown.

Comparing by remembering "how it used to be" is very cruel. Each individual has his or her own strengths and weaknesses. Where one person is strong, the other may be weak, and vice versa. Let your wife live her own life, and don't try to fit her into a mold of what you think she ought to be!

Before I ever met my wife I asked God to please help me not to compare. Comparing will only bring torment to you and hurt to your new bride.

I don't have the cure-all, fix-it-once-and-for-all solution for a happy home and second marriage, but I have briefly discussed its foundation. Any other problems or gray areas that come up can be handled on the same basis, that is, the foundation of love. Together you can press toward the mark. Shoot for the stars from this spring-board.

God so loved that He gave. Likewise give yourself unselfishly to make your home a happy one. Just like bread cast out on the waters of life, your love will come back to you in the form of a loving wife and children.

♥.♥.♥.♥.♥.♥.♥.♥.♥.♥.♥.*12*.♥.

Learning from Others

The idea for this chapter came one day as I sat reading my Bible. As I absorbed the words of Titus 2:3-5 I felt impressed that I wanted to learn from women who have successful marriages.

Because a woman is not in a marriage identical to mine does not mean I can't learn from her. If a woman has been happily married for many years, she has the keys to success in her hand.

Several successful women have fulfilled the command of Titus 2:3: "[Let] the aged [experienced] women likewise . . . be . . . teachers of good things."

First, let me introduce you to my mother. I have lived in her home, and there is no doubt in my mind that my parents are very much in love. My parents enjoy their time together and are best friends. Thank you, Naomi Powers, for sharing these secrets to success:

"Ladies, it takes so little for you to make your husband happy, to make him feel loved and wanted. Yet, so much of the time a woman waits for the man to make her happy. In wanting to get his attention, she places great demands on him.

"If you want to get your husband's attention, you should do little things for him. You will get his attention by looking nice when he comes home from work, by cooking his favorite dinner, or making his favorite dessert. Men do not respond to whining, nagging women. If you want your husband to show you attention with love, you must respond to his needs.

"Make your home pleasant. Is your house clean? Are the children well behaved? Are you there with a cheerful and loving welcome when he comes home? Do you speak with kindness?

"You can have a marriage like millions of others—average—or you can have a beautiful, exciting marriage. It is up to you!"

Sister Nona Freeman and I were discussing this same topic as we made the long drive to Cape May for our ladies retreat. As I drove down the winding roads, enjoying the radiant sunshine and cool breeze blowing in through the open window, I listened as Sister Freeman shared with me her secret for a successful marriage:

"Cindy, after fifty years of marriage we still hold hands. I believe that the successful marriage has this: mutual forgiving of everyday irritants. Learn to forgive without being asked to. When your husband does something thoughtless, say in your mind right then, I forgive you, and put it out of your mind."

The next woman who has so graciously shared with

us is a well-known author, Joy Haney. Her books on marriage and children have blessed and encouraged many. She says:

"Your home is a trust designed by God. A good marriage cannot be bought; it must be nurtured. Christian marriages are an example to the world of the relationship between Christ and the church. On your part as a wife you can be a nag or a hag—hateful, argumentive, and gossipy—or you can be stupendously wonderful. You choose what kind of wife you become—a witch or a queen.

"Daily Bible reading, which stores God's wisdom into your brain, and praying in the Holy Ghost are the best insurance for a great marriage. These devotions help you do the things a wife should do—to be kind, to communicate, to be your husband's best friend and lover, to be joyful, optimistic, diligent, and virtuous."

Several years ago, while on the Associate In Missions program assigned to Athens, Greece, I was privileged to work with Missionaries Alan and Valerie Demos. Sister Demos is a great teacher and example of Christian living. Here are her comments:

"The marriage of the Lamb as described in Revelation 19:7 and 21:1, 2, 9 may be the basis for the modern expression, 'a marriage made in heaven.' However, I don't believe our marriages are made in heaven any more than is the marriage of the Lamb! While the Bible emphasizes the unfailing love of Jesus Christ (the groom), it also clearly teaches that His church (the bride) should react to that love in a responsible way. The true church of Jesus Christ is comprised of people who not only believe but also obey, who not only are washed in the blood of the Lamb but also take up the cross to follow Him, and who not only receive the Spirit of Christ but are also led by that Spirit. This all speaks to me of earthly effort as well as heavenly blessing.

"No matter how in love a couple may feel or how certain they are of the will of God for their union, they are bound for many surprises when they decide to marry. A multitude of differences appear almost overnight—differing opinions, ways of doing things, interests, reactions, approaches to problem solving, and so on. In due time, distressing circumstances of life that no one expects to happen to them add to the strains of adjustment to intimate living. It doesn't take long to realize that a strong, lasting, happy marriage comes with a lot of hard work.

"My parents divorced when I was just two years old so I never had the advantage of learning from them firsthand how to (or not to) work around personal differences. I went into my marriage quite unprepared to cope with my own or my husband's feelings about our differences. It seemed very easy to communicate about what we did not like in each other and to make judgments about who was 'better' or who was 'right,' but it was not easy to help each other cope and change for the sake of harmony.

"Amid all the tried and true resources I have used to keep my marriage strong, there is one little power tool I have learned about through hard experience that keeps me more than married; it keeps me happily married! It seems that as soon as I can lovingly *accept* any unpleasant characteristic in my husband, two wonderful things happen. First of all, I am immediately free of my own disappointments and frustrations caused by not accepting a flaw in someone I love. Whether he ever changes or not, I have changed! Instead of praying for power to forgive, I have guarded against the need for it! Instead of there being two problems (his flaw and my negative reaction to it) there is really only one problem! Second of all, it seems that as my pressure to change him lifts and he feels the soothing security of genuine acceptance, he summons his own desire and energy to change in order to please me.

"Granted, acceptance is easier to discuss than to do; it requires humility, patience, and a certain level of selflessness. But after reaping the benefits of its motivating power in dealing with a marriage problem, it is easier to apply it again and again to other problems. And just in case my own experience should fail to remind me of how important it is to accept my husband as he is at any given time, the example of our Lord is ever leading me in the same direction. 'God demonstrates His own love toward us, in that while we were still sinners, Christ died for us' (Romans 5:8, NKJV). Now that's acceptance!"

My good friend, Dayle Shockley, shared her key for a successful marriage:

"The most important thing for a woman to know in a marriage is how to be submissive to her husband. This came the hardest for me, and as a result of my own stubbornness, I brought a lot of hardships on myself. If I could start over, I would be submissive from the beginning.

"What is submission? According to the dictionary, it is 'to yield oneself to the authority or will of another' or 'to be humble and compliant.' It is knowing when to keep your mouth shut and knowing when to open your arms. It is understanding that God created the man totally different in his emotions from the woman. It is realizing that by God's plan the man should be the leader in your relationship. It is the will of God and it is right. This does not mean that a woman is supposed to be run over or abused by her husband. It simply means that you, the woman, must make your husband feel in control. When you treat your husband in the manner God intended, by being kind, respectful, and gentle, your husband will treat you properly. I know, because I've tried it."

One day in conversation with Stan's former mother-in-law, she shared with me these thoughts on ruling the spirit:

"People think that Proverbs 16:32 only refers to temper when it says 'he that ruleth his spirit,' but ruling your spirit could be controlling temper, bitterness, anger, a martyr complex (self-pity), or strife. You must rule your spirit and produce cheerfulness and kindness."

My uncle, Reverend Nelson Neyland, says in his marriage classes, "The better marriage you have, the better Christian you make."

♥.♥.♥.♥.♥.♥.♥.♥.♥.♥.♥.♥.*13.*

In Conclusion

*O*nce upon a time there lived a potter, a potter who was famous for the beautiful vases that he could so skillfully form upon his wheel.

One day the king of the land commissioned him to create a vase. This vase would grace the king's banquet table, and it had to be a one-of-a-kind masterpiece.

The potter saw in his mind the vase he would create for the king. He picked his clay carefully, and with a vision in his head he began to work. Putting the clay upon his wheel, he began to mold it with his hands, shaping it to match the vision in his mind.

The hours passed and the frustration of the skillful potter mounted. The clay was not molding into a vase as he had planned. Lumps of hard clay had to be removed; therefore, the large ornate vase was becoming smaller. Finally, the disappointed potter stood up from his wheel, but in his hand was not the masterpiece he had so joyfully envisioned as he had set to work. Instead, in his hand was a very small bowl. It was not beautiful. It was not a masterpiece. It would never grace the king's banquet table.

Marriages are meant to be beautiful masterpieces, but with every disagreement not forgiven, with every hurt not forgotten, without compassion for each other, and without compromise in difficult situations, lumps are formed in the clay.

What do you want for your marriage? Are your hurts and disappointments worth holding onto even though it will mean the loss of a "masterpiece" marriage?

It does not matter what people say or do. You are the only one who can give permission for negative, hurtful thoughts to stay in your mind. Not only can you allow them to stay, but you can nurture those thoughts until your mind is a comfortable home for them to live in forever. But if you want a masterpiece marriage you must learn to pray as David did when he cried to the Lord, "Let the words of my mouth, and the meditation of my heart, be acceptable in thy sight, O LORD, my strength, and my redeemer" (Psalm 19:14). You must also cry out to the Lord when painful or angry thoughts come to you, "Lord, let every word that I say and every thought that I think today please you."

Allow the Lord to free you from the chains of wrong attitudes and the dirtiness of a bad spirit. In Psalm 51:10 David prayed, "Create in me a clean heart, O God; and renew a right spirit within me."

It is never too late to change, to accomplish, to overcome. What is one year or three years or even ten years compared to the rest of your life?

It is never too late to create a masterpiece. Michelangelo completed the dome of St. Peter's at the age of seventy. Sophocles wrote *Oedipus Tyrannus* at the age of eighty. Pablo Casals was giving cello concerts at age eighty-eight. You, too, have a beautiful masterpiece to create. I challenge you to put aside every excuse and start today!